Visions of Utopia
in Switzerland

Occasional Papers in Swiss Studies

edited by
Joy Charnley and Malcolm Pender

Centre for Swiss Cultural Studies

Volume 3

PETER LANG
Oxford • Bern • Berlin • Bruxelles • Frankfurt a.M. • New York • Wien

Joy Charnley, Malcolm Pender (eds)

Visions of Utopia
in Switzerland

PETER LANG

Oxford • Bern • Berlin • Bruxelles • Frankfurt a.M. • New York • Wien

Die Deutsche Bibliothek – CIP-Einheitsaufnahme

Visions of Utopia in Switzerland : Joy Charnley / Malcolm Pender (ed.). –
Oxford ; Bern ; Berlin ; Bruxelles ; Frankfurt a.M. ; New York ; Wien :
Lang, 2000
(Occasional papers in Swiss studies ; Vol. 3)
ISBN 3-906766-64-0

British Library and Library of Congress Cataloguing-in-Publication Data:
A catalogue record for this book is available from *The British Library,* Great
Britain, and from *The Library of Congress,* USA

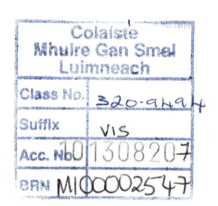

ISSN 1423-9825
ISBN 3-906766-64-0
US-ISBN 0-8204-5336-6

© Peter Lang AG, European Academic Publishers, Bern 2000
Jupiterstr. 15, Postfach, 3000 Bern 15, Switzerland;
info@peterlang.com; www.peterlang.net

Printed in Germany

Contents

Introduction

Long before the concept of 'Utopia' was formulated by Sir Thomas More in the sixteenth century, the vision of an ideal society had begun to fascinate human beings and, in real and imaginary journeys to far-off lands, writers told of the ways in which other societies organised themselves and dealt with central issues such as religion, education and work. Utopia, as depicted by More, was an imaginary island possessing an ideal social, legal and political system. Certainly, Switzerland is perceived by others as an island of peace in times of European war and of prosperity in times of European peace, and by the Swiss as an island of doughty self-determination on a factious continent. This Swiss self-perception derives very directly from a view of 1291, the year of the revolt against the Habsburgs. Yet the larger part of More's definition might be covered to a considerable extent by an achievement seemingly accorded less mythical status by the Swiss, the constitutional reform of 1848 which created the present political structures and legal system, and which was, incidentally the one shining success in that dark year of political failure in Europe. The manner of achieving the reform, a difficult compromise of political, religious and economic differences eventually sanctioned by popular vote, bordered on the ideal in the regulation of human affairs. The outcome of the reform, the Constitution of 1848, has been adjusted over the years in the light of changing circumstances – the last such adjustment coming into force at the beginning of the new millennium – and this flexibility constitutes a recognition that there must be ceaseless forward movement towards an ideal. Arguably, the political arrangements which enable the cultures of Switzerland to live together in relative harmony can be viewed in the year 2000, when Europe remains scarred by repression and violence between ethnic and language groups, as being closer to Utopia than arrangements obtaining in other places.

The essays in this third volume of *Occasional Papers in Swiss Studies* discuss differing notions of Utopia in relation to Switzerland and the often chastening confrontation of these notions with reality: the view of writers of the Swiss Enlightenment on the ideal social composition of their country, in the twentieth century the perceptions of Jewish refugees and foreign migrant workers of Switzerland as a political or economic haven, the construction of an ideal modern city, the historical ideal of self-defence perverted into a vision of society wholly organised on that principle, Utopian concepts for dealing with the increasingly complex organisation of modern society.

At a time when Switzerland is in some doubt about the kind of society she wishes to become — isolationist or open to Europe, narrowly traditional or widely multi-cultural — this volume aims to provide an overview of some of the visions offered. Since, in the past, many ended in disappointment and failure, it remains to be seen what the future holds for the Utopias of the twenty-first century.

We should like to thank both the Department of Modern Languages and the Research and Development Fund of the University of Strathclyde for the financial support which made the publication of this volume possible.

Joy Charnley   University of Strathclyde
Malcolm Pender   Glasgow, December 2000

JOY CHARNLEY

'J'aime bien ma Suisse': Some Italian Reactions to the Schwarzenbach Initiative of 1970

Viewed from the poorer regions of Southern Europe, the Switzerland of the late 1940s certainly appeared to be something of an economic paradise, offering an escape from poverty and deprivation. As for the Swiss, the easy availability of workers for building sites and hotels suited them very well and in 1948 the first intergovernmental agreement was signed with Italy. As a result, although in the first half of the century the percentage of foreigners living in Switzerland actually fell (from 15.4 per cent in 1914 to 5.2 per cent in 1941) from the 1950s onwards it has on the whole steadily climbed.[1] Despite the introduction of quotas for the first time in 1963, the number of resident foreigners (many of them, it must be remembered, fairly well-off and long established) has increased from 285,000 in 1950 to 1,100,000 in 1999 and having made up 10.8 per cent of the population in 1960 and 17.2 per cent in 1973 this proportion has now reached close on 20 per cent.[2]

It has been claimed that 'la vague latine des Italiens et Espagnols des années 50 et 60 constitue l'une des vagues d'immigration les plus importantes de l'histoire suisse'[3] but since the 1980s new immigrants have tended to come from countries such as Yugoslavia, Zaïre and Turkey. Reactions to the different generations of immigrants have however been remarkably similar in many ways; as one group has become better accepted

1   Blaise Lempen, *Un modèle en crise* (Lausanne: 1985), p. 74. Numbers did however fall back to 14 per cent in 1980 after the oil crisis of the 1970s; see Marc Vuilleumier, *Immigrés et réfugiés en Suisse* (Pro Helvetia: 1987), p. 85.

2   See the dossier entitled '50 ans d'immigration', in *L'Histoire*, février 1999, pp. 33–61 (p. 39), Lempen, p. 74 and Jonathan Steinberg, *Why Switzerland?* Second edition (Cambridge: 1996), p. 125. This percentage can be usefully compared with the figures recorded in other European countries: 2.5 per cent in Denmark, 7 per cent in France and 25 per cent in Luxembourg.

3   Lempen, p. 74.

others have arrived to take their place and 'aliens who were looked upon as a threat a generation ago belong to us today'.[4] In the 1950s, too, many Swiss forgot that if these workers were there it was because Swiss industry both wanted and needed them and a desire to reject, exclude and scapegoat was unfortunately more often in evidence than efforts to accept and integrate and such attitudes can still be witnessed today.[5]

The long history of these reactions in Switzerland can be traced back to the early years of the twentieth century and a group of writers known as the 'Helvétistes'. These intellectuals were writers such as Gonzague de Reynold, Robert de Traz and the Cingria brothers who around 1908 were already developing the types of arguments which were to re-emerge in the 1930s and again in the late sixties and which fed support for the so-called Schwarzenbach Initiative of 1970 as well as for subsequent initiatives. Of them a historian has written:

> [...]perplexes face au fort nombre d'étrangers installés dans le pays, désorientés par des mutations sociales où ils croient discerner les symptômes d'une dégénérescence, nombreux sont les intellectuels suisses qui, en ce début de siècle, s'inquiètent et s'interrogent, à la recherche d'une identité nationale malaisée à définir. [...ils] réfléchissent au meilleur moyen d'intégrer des étrangers dont ils redoutent qu'ils ne dissolvent les moeurs nationales et sont parfois sceptiques face à la démocratie parlementaire qui leur paraît favoriser une 'médiocratie'.[6]

James Schwarzenbach, the initiator, 'un habile petit père tranquille'[7] had a family background which perhaps made his later political activity unsurprising. A member of the Wille-Schwarzenbach clan, his uncle Ulrich Wille II, an admirer of Hitler, was a leading light in the anti-Jenisch campaign instituted by Pro Juventute in 1926 (*Enfants de la Grand' Route*)

---

4   Walter Schmid, 'Immigration', in Rolf Kieser and Kurt R. Spillmann (eds), *The New Switzerland. Problems and Policies* (Palo Alto: 1995), pp. 224–236 (p. 227). See also Vuilleumier, p. 102.

5   Lempen p. 78 and Jacques Pilet, *Le crime nazi de Payerne. 1942, en Suisse: un Juif tué 'pour l'exemple'* (Lausanne: 1977), p. 186. Dieter Fahrni points out for example in *An Outline History of Switzerland. From the Origins to the Present Day* (Pro Helvetia: 1992), p. 119, that approximately 70 per cent of hotel staff are non-Swiss.

6   Alain Clavien, *Les Helvétistes. Intellectuels et politique en Suisse romande au début du siècle* (Lausanne: 1993), p. 7.

7   Pilet, p. 185.

as a result of which 'on a détruit des familles, enlevé plus de 600 enfants à leurs parents, désespéré des mères, anéanti une culture'.[8] Subsequently, inspired like his father by 'sa haine de la France et son amour aveugle pour l'Allemagne'[9] Ulrich Wille II plotted to get Guisan dismissed from his post as General in 1940, and was perhaps encouraged by the example of his father, appointed General during the First World War, who had blatantly disregarded Swiss neutrality.[10] If James attracted the disapproval of his family by converting to Catholicism, in politics he faithfully adopted the 'extrémisme de droite de Wille et de son clan'[11] and was a complete contrast to his cousin Annemarie Schwarzenbach whose left-wing friends Klaus and Erika Mann he insulted and denounced. His openly expressed pleasure in 1942 at the defeat of France was once again a clear indication of where his sympathies lay.[12] In 1967 Schwarzenbach joined the right-wing party *Nationale Aktion* which had been created in 1961 and quickly became its President. Following disagreements however he left the party to found his 'Republican' movement in 1970.

Thus Schwarzenbach's background contained a series of elements which could quite logically lead to the initiative as conceived by him, notably right-wing extremism, anti-democratic opinions and intolerance of difference. His view, put simply, was that different cultures and mentalities could not coexist, that Switzerland was threatened by an excessive number of foreigners, essentially Italians and Spaniards, who had to return to their homelands. Propaganda manipulated some people's fear of difference and their feeling of being dominated by foreigners and constructed a myth of 'pureté patriotique', a never-changing perfect

---

8   Nicolas Meienberg, *Le délire général. L'Armée suisse sous influence,* translated by
     Monique Picard (Genève: 1988), p. 26. Published in German by Limmat Verlag in
     1987. For personal testimony of the effects of this policy see Mariella Mehr,
     'Switzerland and the Gypsies' in Mitya New, *Switzerland Unwrapped. Exposing
     the Myths* (London: 1997), pp. 110–17.
9   Meienberg, p. 15.
10   Meienberg, pp. 24–5, pp. 129–30.
11   Meienberg, p. 130. See also p. 37 for details of an incident involving Schwarzenbach's
     father Edwin.
12   Meienberg, p. 111. On Annemarie Schwarzenbach (1908–1942) see Meienberg pp.
     101–11 and the Postface by Roger Perret in Ella Maillart, *La voie cruelle* (Lausanne:
     1987), pp. 224–39.

Switzerland where all would be well if only there were fewer foreigners.[13] Southern Europeans were singled out for exclusion just as the Jews had been in some countries on many occasions.[14]

Known officially in French as the 'initiative contre l'emprise et la surpopulation étrangères' the initiative put to the people on 7 June 1970 (the second of several) thus proposed the forced departure within four years of 400,000 immigrants, the percentage of foreigners in each canton not to exceed 10 per cent (except for Geneva, where the situation was necessarily different due to the high number of diplomats and international officials and where a figure of 25 per cent was suggested). Preference was to be given to 'saisonniers', seasonal workers who would have no right to permanent residence and whose permits would not be renewed if the economy faltered. After an extremely vigorous campaign on both sides and a particularly high turnout of 74.7 per cent (of male voters only obviously, since women did not gain the federal vote until the following year!) the result was closer than some would have liked: 46 per cent in favour, 54 per cent against and less than 100,000 votes separated the two camps.[15] Seven of the then twenty-two cantons had said 'yes' to the initiative, with a high of 63 per cent in Uri, a rural canton not noted for its high immigrant population. Perhaps logically, the lowest percentage in favour was recorded in Italian-speaking Ticino, although even there 36 per cent of voters agreed with the proposition.[16]

These results were particularly striking for at least two reasons. Firstly, Schwarzenbach had been the only member of parliament to vote in favour of his own initiative and hence the people's not inconsiderable support underlined a divide between electors and elected. Secondly, given the

---

13   For examples of the depths plumbed and the opinions expressed by readers and others in newspapers, see Hubert Auque, *L'étranger qui fait exister la Suisse. Contribution psychanalytique à l'étude sociologique de la place de l'étranger dans la société suisse* (Perpignan: 1981), pp. 184–221.

14   Pilet, p. 186. For details of the succession of events leading up to the initiative see Pierre Fiala and Marianne Ebel, *Langages xénophobes et consensus national en Suisse (1960-80)* (Lausanne: 1983), pp. 21–31 and on Schwarzenbach, pp. 48–54.

15   G. Andrey et al, *Nouvelle Histoire de la Suisse et des Suisses,* 3 vols (Lausanne: 1983), III, p. 240.

16   For the full list of results, canton by canton, see Jean-Jacques Bouquet, *Histoire de la Suisse,* Collection 'Que sais-je?' (Paris: 1995), p. 122.

universal opposition to the initiative amongst politicians, the closeness of the result was somewhat surprising since it could have been expected that political parties would have more impact on the outcome. It certainly seems fair to conclude that it was ultimately economic rather than moral issues which won the day:

> Si la classe politique ne l'avait pas condamnée, si la crainte d'une crise économique profonde n'avait pas fait réfléchir, l'initiative aurait pu obtenir le plus grand nombre de suffrages.[17]

The closeness of the result led to a reinforcement of the right-wing movement and encouraged its members to pursue their goal. Further initiatives were however not successful, including one launched by *Nationale Aktion* which in October 1974 again achieved a high turnout of 69.6 per cent, almost 900,000 electors voting for it. Despite this succession of defeats for the far right and its loss of support in recent years, other 'victories' point to the continued presence of a certain current of ideas: for example the refusal by voters in 1981 to accord an improved status to seasonal workers, proposals rejected by a massive 83.8 per cent, or the rejection in 1994 of a proposition which would have brought into existence a process of 'naturalisation facilitée' for young foreigners.[18] Thus even if it is the case that 'sur le plan électoral, les partis xénophobes, affaiblis par des dissensions internes, ont fortement reculé' they are still present in Swiss society and have now switched their attention from Southern Europeans to immigrants from developing nations.[19]

   This, then, was the situation and a particular type of reaction to the arrival in Switzerland of large numbers of foreign workers over two decades or so of postwar economic growth. What, on the opposite side, were the reactions of some of those Italian workers who were on the receiving end of this prejudice? Anne Cuneo (1936), an Italian (now Swiss) who first

17   Lempen, p. 20.
18   On 1981 see Fiala/Ebel, p. 429. In 1994 53 per cent of voters accepted the proposition but since a majority was only achieved in ten cantons, it fell short of the required 'double majorité'. See Steinberg, p. 126.
19   Bouquet, p. 123. Indeed, the seventh anti-foreigner initiative since the Second World War, 'für eine Regelung der Zuwanderung' is currently being prepared; see Martin Furrer, 'Aufruf zur Abwehrschlacht', *Die Weltwoche*, 49, 3 December 1998, pp. 19–20.

arrived in Switzerland after the War, wrote *La Vermine*, which is set in the Vaud and is closely based on events surrounding the Schwarzenbach Initiative between November 1969 and January 1970, that is shortly before the vote took place.[20] Her account thus represents the point of view of someone living through the events in question and possibly, given the results (41 per cent of *vaudois* voters replied 'yes'), fearing that the initiative might succeed. It is a work of fiction inspired by reality and was produced by a writer who by 1970 had already published two autobiographical works.[21] This sets it in contrast with another two books which both also involve Italian women living in the canton of Vaud, but which are 'récits de vie' or 'témoignages' rather than fictional accounts.[22] Neither of these concentrates exclusively on the initiative but each gives the viewpoint of someone who has experienced life as a foreigner in Switzerland and hence known prejudice at first hand; in addition both are women who are not writers but have had the help of a 'professional' in putting together their accounts.

'*La Vermine* ne veut pas être un "acte littéraire"' we are told on the back cover, meaning that it is political and 'engagé' rather than pure literature. Cuneo's grounding in reality is made immediately evident by the dedication 'à la mémoire de Attilio Tonola assassiné à St-Moritz le 23 novembre 1968 par trois ivrognes qui "n'aiment pas les Italiens" et que les Tribunaux ont laissés en liberté' but she insists that her story is only 'un avenir possible', it remains a 'fable', a 'fable-fiction', in which 'rien n'est réel'. Such protestations are of course amply contradicted by the many details 'borrowed' from reality which are disseminated throughout the text: the story obviously takes place in Lausanne (the *Grand Pont* being transformed into the *Pont Majeur*), the names of several Federal Councillors have been adapted (von Moos/Stoos) and the picture of an economy dependant on foreign labour to run its restaurants and petrol stations is clearly drawn. There are references to a certain 'Schwarzwald' and indications that the story is set after the success of an anti-foreigner

---

20 Lausanne: 1970.
21 The works in question were *Gravé au diamant* (Lausanne: 1967) and *Mortelle maladie* (Lausanne: 1969) in which Cuneo already speaks about her experiences as a foreigner in Switzerland.
22 Carla Belotti/Claire Masnata-Rubattel, *L'Emigrée* (Genève: 1981) and Sylviane Roche/Marie-Rose De Donno, *L'Italienne* (Orbe: 1998).

initiative: the central character reflects that 'il a eu raison de voter comme il l'a fait' (p. 19) and another comments, 'vous voyez maintenant combien nous avions raison de nous méfier. On en a renvoyé quatre cent mille' (p. 52). Cuneo also includes some 'clins d'oeil' at specific Swiss targets, such as the central character Bolomet's outrage at not being treated as he expects – 'vous manquez de respect à un officier suisse' (p. 40) – or the reference to his generous donations to Pro Juventute. Given the association's involvement in the controversial *Enfants de la Grand' Route* programme and, as noted above, the political views of some of its patrons, the irony of such protestations becomes clear:

> Xénophobes! Les Suisses! Et qui a fondé la Croix-Rouge? [...] Il .[Bolomet] donne, lui, il donne toujours. Il donne aussi pour Pro Juventute et autres Pro. (p. 26)

The title, *La Vermine*, is clearly intended to have multiple meanings, one of which is indicated by the inclusion of a quotation from the beginning of Kafka's *Metamorphosis*, 'un matin, au sortir d'un rêve agité, Grégoire Samsa s'éveilla transformé dans son lit en une véritable vermine'.[23] Just like Gregor Samsa, people have overnight been turned into 'vermine', not just the deported Italians who have now become 'persona non grata' but also Jacques Bolomet and other Swiss who have allowed their minds to be taken over by the 'vermine' represented by the ideas of 'Schwarzwald'. Just like Samsa, Bolomet is thrown into the situation unawares, having just returned from a trip to the USSR, where he has had no news from Switzerland and just as in *Metamorphosis*, the story begins with the central character waking up in the morning and sensing fairly soon that all is not well. Finally, and more prosaically, literal vermin proliferate in the book, since as time goes on and rubbish is not collected, all the workers who used to do the job having returned to Italy, the city starts to have a problem with rats and Jacques has to circumvent piles of rubbish when he leaves home (pp. 75–6).

The situation is described entirely through the experiences and thoughts of Jacques Bolomet, whose name immediately identifies him as a typical *Vaudois*. Early on, we learn that he has racist opinions and voted for the initiative and yet, paradoxically, he lives and works with Italians

23   *La Métamorphose,* translated by Alexandre Vialatte (Paris: 1976), p. 5.

and many of his activities, indeed his daily existence, become impossible once they are longer there – the building site which he is in charge of grinds to a halt, he can no longer get a pizza at lunchtime, he risks running out of petrol since several garages have had to close. All these jobs had been done by people who were almost invisible for him and whose importance he had ignored and he is incapable of seeing the fundamental contradiction between the views he expresses and the life he leads. His dependence is not just economic, however; he had, in spite of his views, married (or been tricked into marrying, as he subsequently sees it) an Italian woman who has left for Italy, presumably to take part in the revolution which has broken out there. Although he rails against her, realising now how he has been duped, his domestic incompetence is quickly revealed. Just as the Swiss economy exploited cheap labour, so in the home men such as he are unaware of their dependence upon women and both economically and domestically Switzerland cannot cope without foreigners:

> Je suis suisse, je vous assure, c'est parce que ma femme, une étrangère, m'a abandonné que je suis comme vous me voyez. Qui cirerait mes souliers? Qui brosserait mes habits? Qui ravauderait mes chaussettes?
>
> (p. 79)

However, Bolomet's intolerance does not stop at Italians and in order to complete the picture we are given a lot of evidence of his dislike and mistrust for German- and Italian-speaking Swiss. Thus, if Italians are 'métèques' (p. 29), 'Nègre[s]' (p. 75) who 'sont docteurs et tout le tremblement seulement parce qu'ils savent lire' (p. 19), a *Tessinois* he had encountered during his studies and who had had the temerity to do better than him in exams is considered as 'presque étranger' (p. 61) whereas a Swiss-German is swiftly categorised as 'borné, comme tous les Suisses-toto' (p. 24). Bolomet is thus a mouthpiece for intolerance and prejudice, he openly expresses the racist clichés which many might share and brings out into the open the views which opponents to the initiative in 1970 were precisely seeking to combat. Cuneo allows him to occupy centre-stage and rather than being opposed by other characters it is the excessive and stereotypical nature of his views and the absurdity of the situation which provide a contradiction to his words.

The deportation of 400,000 Italians, followed by the outbreak of a revolution in Italy, which means that even more Italians have left (especially the seasonal workers, upon whom Switzerland is now dependent), leads to a complete breakdown and despite the reassuring words of the Swiss President (pp. 31–3), Lausanne is in turmoil. People are quickly divided into two camps – for or against foreigners – and a resistance group known as the 'hirsutes' organises help and support for persecuted non-Swiss and interrupts the radio messages by Federal Councillors with its own calls for solidarity (pp. 65–6). Bolomet is incredulous that Swiss people could possibly want to support such a movement and is distressed that his unkempt appearance leads him to be mistaken for a 'hirsute'. Despite the help unwittingly afforded him by the resistants, who think he is one of them, he has no wish to change camps and refuses the opportunity to question his prejudices. He is incapable of thinking logically and of realising that it is ridiculous to make differences between people on the basis of appearance (which can change according to circumstances) or because of a passport (which can be lost).

Bolomet is obviously not alone in his opinions and Cuneo gives an idea of the deep-rooted, unreflecting racist views which exist in Swiss society through encounters with other characters. The racist mob which attacks Bolomet when he is mistaken for a foreigner (p. 82) is perhaps a standard element in this type of narrative, as is the tendency even to blame the Italians for the ugly buildings built to house them (p. 29) but the standpoint of a trade unionist is less expected. He declares opposition to the anti-foreigner action but not because it is morally wrong, rather because he believes that workers established in Switzerland will be easier to control and manipulate than 'saisonniers' and he reassures Bolomet that 'nous n'aimons pas plus que vous ces espèces d'Arabes qu'on nous envoie depuis quelques années' (p. 52). This displays a clear lack of solidarity between Swiss and non-Swiss workers and fits in with the argument expressed earlier according to which it was economic rather than moral factors which carried the most weight when people made up their minds; for many the proposition in itself was not shocking, it was simply a question of deciding what the impact on jobs and financial security would be.

Ultimately, Cuneo's conclusion is pessimistic: Bolomet does not change and despite his experiences he does not begin to think differently or question any of his assumptions. The final chapter starts with the phrases which figure at the very beginning of the book (p. 117), creating the impression that nothing has changed, apart from Bolomet's job: he is now clearly a member of the police force or army in charge of rooting out dissidents and the final sentence, 'il a beaucoup à faire aujourd'hui, au Pont Majeur' (p. 119) is full of menace. He has confirmed his allegiance to the xenophobes whose intolerance, one senses, can only get worse; a 'paysanne' at the market for example reacts to the suggestion of bringing in Tunisians or South Africans to work in certain jobs with a terse, 'c'était déjà dur avec les Italiens, alors quand ce sera plein de Nègres' (p. 103). Unlike in Kafka's *Metamorphosis* where Samsa dies and 'normality' returns to the family, here the 'vermine' are victorious, they thrive and proliferate rather than being eliminated in spite of Cuneo's final ironic 'la petite place devant la maison a retrouvé sa propreté d'antan' (p. 119). The consequences of the mass expulsion of foreigners are thus portrayed as being entirely negative: increasing hatred and division, the collapse of the economy, deep tensions within society and the domination of sinister right-wing forces which are laws unto themselves. Cuneo's warning is clear and uncompromising.

The 'invisible' workers Jacques Bolomet so dislikes and whose voices we do not hear in *La Vermine* have found the opportunity to express themselves in 'récits de vie' such as *L'émigrée* (1981) and *L'Italienne* (1998).[24] In these accounts two Italian women describe their lives and experiences of domestic service and shop work, providing insight into the world of Italian workers in Switzerland from the 1950s onwards. Carla Belotti's account of her life, written in 1981 in collaboration with Claire Masnata-Rubattel, describes the author's poor childhood in Italy, her discovery of life in Switzerland and the reality of being considered differently because one is a foreigner. Born in 1924, Carla is attracted to Switzerland by the possibility of finding work and the higher salaries, going first, after the War, to the Ticino where, she says, 'je n'ai jamais souffert d'être étrangère' (p. 64) and then to Vaud where things were different:

---

24   In her Introduction to *Femmes écrivains suisses de langue française. Solitude surpeuplée*, second edition (Lausanne: 1997), Doris Jakubec comments on women's particular fondness for the process of 'témoignage' through 'récits de vie' (p. 17). She remarks that such accounts 'fleurissent aux périodes déboussolées, lourdes de menaces et de questions inquiètes sur les choix de société'.

> [...] il n'y a pas de doute que, parce que j'étais étrangère, j'étais moins considérée. Je sentais que l'on me traitait en étrangère. Et je le sens maintenant encore. [...] bien que je sois suisse, maintenant, je me sens encore un peu étrangère. (p. 109)

Carla Belotti describes very clearly the contribution made by Italian workers to the Swiss economy, giving lively and often highly critical comment on her successive 'patrons' and declaring that 'il ne faut pas dire que l'argent que la Suisse a donné aux étrangers, elle l'a donné sans les faire suer' (p. 148). The death of one brother and serious accident of another, who loses a leg and has to return to Italy, are certainly vivid examples of the price paid by such workers (p. 133). They escape poverty but the cost, in terms of personal loss and sacrifice, is high. Although she remarks that when younger she did not realise that 'notre révolte personnelle avait des causes sociales' (p. 64), Belotti points out that 'c'est facile de renvoyer les gens, [...] après les avoir exploités aussi longtemps qu'on en avait besoin' (p. 148–9) and she draws attention to the vulnerable nature of seasonal workers, those who have 'le permis A', precisely the category which the Schwarzenbach Initiative proposed to rely upon (p. 149).

Frightened by what she calls 'les initiatives Schwarzenbach' (p. 144), mentioned several times, she and her husband decided to request Swiss nationality for 'on avait peur d'être expulsés et de devoir laisser notre petit chalet où on avait mis toutes nos économies'. She has visions of Schwarzenbach himself coming in person to repossess their chalet:

> [...] je ne veux pas être expulsée par Schwarzenbach et le laisser prendre notre chalet; nous avons fait des sacrifices, il n'y a pas de raison de le laisser entrer et de nous faire mettre dehors. (p. 145)

The process of naturalisation, although eventually successful, is a difficult experience for her and one which leaves her feeling humiliated. She is however entirely aware of the absurdity of some of the questions asked and pertinently remarks that 'l'histoire suisse, même les Suisses ne la savent pas tous; pas seulement les étrangers' (p. 147). Through her criticism of Switzerland and the Swiss and the less than flattering portrait which she gives on occasions, Carla Belotti provides a clear picture of the sacrifices and struggles of workers such as her and ample contradiction of the claims of xenophobes such as 'Bolomet'. Her views from the ground are a useful antidote to the racist venom reproduced in *La Vermine* and her optimistic conclusion after many years of hard work – 'je ne veux pas jeter la pierre à la Suisse. J'aime bien ma Suisse' (p. 149) – is encouraging and hopeful in contrast to Cuneo's pessimism.

Sylviane Roche's account of the life of Marie-Rose De Donno, *L'Italienne,* in Roche's words 'une oeuvre commune', is once again a personal 'témoignage', providing anecdotal experience rather than political or social analysis. Like Belotti, De Donno begins with her impoverished childhood, this time in the very south of Italy, and recounts more or less chronologically the events which have so far marked her existence. The two women have worked together to tell 'l'histoire d'une vie' in which the interdependency between Switzerland and poor Italians – the former in need of workers, the latter seeking to escape poverty – is constantly present. Born in 1950, De Donno first comes into contact with Switzerland in 1957 when her mother has to leave behind her own children to go to the *Valais* to look after someone else's (p. 19). Too young to work herself and therefore of no interest to her mother's employers, De Donno is unable to stay permanently in Switzerland and is separated from her mother for long periods, an experience shared by many thousands of children of seasonal workers. She divides her time between the two countries for several years and thus begins the 'va-et-vient' between north and south which even in adulthood was to be an established pattern for her since 'il n'avait jamais été question qu'on reste en Suisse, qu'on s'y fixe' (p. 105). She describes in vivid terms her memories of the masses of Italian workers fighting for seats on the train taking them to Switzerland – 'on aurait dit qu'ils partaient pour [...] un endroit merveilleux [...] Mais il partaient juste travailler en Suisse' (p. 23) – and recalls that for her at that stage it was a place which represented little more than 'la bouffe' (p. 37), 'un pays où les gens mangeaient même le soir! C'était absolument épatant' (p. 25).

De Donno speaks very clearly about the economic vulnerability of Italian workers in the 1950s and 1960s, a vulnerability which of course would have been increased by those who proposed in the 1970s to rely heavily upon 'saisonniers' rather than give foreign workers the right to permanent residence. Such workers, with limited rights and subject to potentially unfair decisions, could easily find themselves out of a job or be obliged to work *au noir* and without insurance; in addition they often (like De Donno and her mother) found it difficult to find somewhere decent to live, either through lack of resources or simply because they were Italian. She also gives examples of the insidious *sexual* exploitation of which women in particular were sometimes victims: first her mother, who 'a dû coucher avec certains hommes pour qu'on ait à manger' (p. 27) and who slept with her boss because 'elle y était pratiquement obligée, à cause du permis de travail, c'était un vrai chantage' (p. 50) and then herself, abused and raped shortly after her arrival in Switzerland as a child, her protests being met with 'on croirait qui, la petite fille ou le policier?' (p. 48) or 'c'est moi qu'on va croire parce que je suis âgé, respectable' (p. 55). Her status as the child of a foreign worker obviously made her particularly defenceless and although she does not evoke political issues such as the Schwarzenbach Initiative she does refer to the negative reactions to Italians in Switzerland and mentions some of the more common criticisms, such as the inevitable 'les Italiens étaient très mal vus. Les gens disaient qu'on était sales' (p. 53).

Although living in Switzerland thus means hard work, loneliness or even trauma for her – as with Belotti, death, this time that of her son, is a sombre presence here (p. 196) – the country comes to represent freedom and independence, whereas Italy offers an easy family life but at the cost of her hard-earned autonomy. De Donno's account illustrates well the broad spectrum of work done in Switzerland by women such as her in shops and hospitals and moves one to reflect once again on the importance of all these 'invisible' workers. She herself dwells relatively little on these experiences but her initiative, drive, ability and overwhelming desire to 'ne pas retomber dans la misère' (p. 225), traits doubtless shared by many of her compatriots, are impressive.

Two opposing visions are thus here confronted: on the one hand the society which Schwarzenbach and those who agreed with him aimed to create by excluding large numbers of people and on the other the multicultural society which Italians, amongst others, wished to join. As Belotti makes clear, the 'membership fee' set by this society, involving hard work and sacrifice, was relatively high; contrary to widely held beliefs, immigrants from Southern Europe indeed worked hard to earn their place and, as we have seen, their contribution to the Swiss economy was considerable, helping the country for example to double its GNP between

1950 and 1973.[25] Switzerland thus represented a strangely paradoxical utopia for Italians; whilst it provided work and a way out of poverty it also expected to get its 'money's worth' in return and did not easily accept newcomers.

It seems that the ideas defended by politicians such as Schwarzenbach fade into the background from time to time only to re-emerge 'à chaque fois que les clameurs du monde apportent plus d'angoisses que d'espoirs'[26] – at the beginning of the century, during the 1930s and again in the 1970s for example. Their influence goes deep, impregnating Swiss society with 'des valeurs obsidionales et des mythes alpestres dont les Suisses ont aujourd'hui encore de la peine à se défaire'.[27] Each epoch has its scapegoats, whether they be political refugees or workers, fleeing persecution or destitution, Jews, Southern Europeans or those from further afield. Each generation continues to judge harshly those who for whatever reason seek refuge within the Swiss borders and the tendency to assume that immigrants cost Switzerland vast sums of money is still widespread.[28]

Some of those specifically targeted by the Schwarzenbach Initiative of 1970 have made an important contribution to the history of Switzerland by adding their voices and experiences to the debate around the composition of the population and the merits or demerits of 'multiculturalism'. Cuneo, an educated woman, writing 'à chaud', gives a vivid, one might say apocalyptic portrayal of what Switzerland's future could have held if anti-foreigner legislation had been passed. In a different kind of account, more personal and less militant, both Belotti and De Donno, members of a non-intellectual 'silent majority', tell their stories, the stories of working women who have encountered prejudice and fought to find a place in Swiss society. Theirs are the voices of the often unheard, the silent mass of workers who did low status jobs which kept the economy going. Covering a period of

---

25   Vuilleumier, p. 94.
26   Pilet, p. 185.
27   Clavien, p. 300.
28   In a recent survey, for instance, when asked how much a refugee cost Switzerland per day, the average response was 164.70SF, whereas in reality the figure is 41SF. Those surveyed were equally uninformed about the amount of 'pocket money' given to refugees, the average answer (22.40SF) being way above the real figure of 3SF. See Pierre-André Stauffer, 'Sommes-nous prêts à accueillir les Kosovars?' *L'Hebdo*, 17, 29 April 1999, 18-23.

almost thirty years from 1970 to 1998, these three works give important insight into the views of those who could potentially have figured amongst the 400,000 Italians deported in *La Vermine* and stand testimony to the enduring nature of prejudice as well as the need for tolerance and mutual understanding.

BERNARD DEGEN

The Total Defence Society:
A Dark Vision of the Political and Military Elite

Until recently there was a view of society abroad in Switzerland which should not merely have surprised but also angered enlightened citizens in the late twentieth century. And it was by no means simply pub talk. The Federal Council, the government of the country, itself stated in a message to Parliament as late as the spring of 1988: 'Das Wort, "die Schweiz hat keine Armee, sie ist eine Armee" beschreibt eine Realität, die im Ausland immer wieder Bewunderung erweckt'.[1] This view was also repeatedly put forward in the press and in books.[2] In the 1980s, however, it was – depending on your political point of view – either a dream or a bitter irony. Yet it is remarkable that such an oddball notion never created a greater fuss in a country which, since 1848, has had a largely unbroken democratic tradition. However, the saying also held good: 'Weder darf die Armee die Demokratie militarisieren, noch ist der Demokratie erlaubt, die Armee zu demokratisieren'.[3] In practice, however, it was never possible to separate clearly the authoritarian nature of the army and the participatory nature of the political system.

In justification of the considerable influence exerted by military attitudes and institutions, there arose from the mid-1960s until the mid-1970s the so-called 'General Defence Concept'. On the one hand, this was part of the context of area planning which was common at the time in relation to actual or anticipated difficulties. Thus it was followed by a general transport concept and a general energy concept.[4] On the other hand,

---

1   'Botschaft über die Volksinitiative "für eine Schweiz ohne Armee und für eine umfassende Friedenspolitik"', 25 May 1988, in *Bundesblatt*, 1988/II, p. 975.

2   Compare Hans Rudolf Kurz (ed), *Die Schweizer Armee heute* (Thun: 1989), p. 432.

3   Kurz, p. 431.

4   Wolf Linder, Beat Holz, Hans Werder, *Planung in der schweizerischen Demokratie* (Bern: 1979), p. 67.

it related to an altogether different context. Whereas with energy or transport policy basically two modern trends were confronting one another, namely the technocratic management of problems of capacity and the ecological demand for careful husbanding of resources, ideas about national defence remained deeply rooted in the thinking of the Second World War. Building on this basis, General Defence was reacting to specific problems of the 1960s, not least to the Utopias for a better society which were gaining ground at the time. As a vision, which was both technocratically neutral and guaranteed by institutions, of a conservative Switzerland, it carried considerable conviction well into the 1980s, especially with older men. In what follows, some of its civilian aspects will be set forth; military considerations will be mentioned only marginally.

The defence doctrine which developed in the course of the 1960s built on escalating notions of 'total war' against the background of the atomic threat. Karl Schmid, a colonel in the General Staff whose main occupation was as Professor of German Language and Literature at the Swiss Federal Institute of Technology in Zürich, and who additionally was an extremely prolific author on military matters, wrote in 1960:

> Die Stärke einer Nation im Krieg ist etwas viel komplexeres als die Summe aus der Stärke des Heeres und der Stärke der Wirtschaft, die sich noch einigermassen in Zahlen bestimmen lassen. Es gibt eine grosse Unbekannte, die diese Summe der militärischen und wirtschaftlichen Kraft entweder vervielfachen oder aber auch gänzlich zunichte machen kann: die seelische Stärke und Widerstandskraft der Nation und im besonderen des Heeres.[5]

According to a widely held view, total war would be waged on these three fronts once it broke out. But:

> Hier steckt ein entscheidender Irrtum: er wird nicht ausbrechen, sondern er ist im Gange. Wir sind im totalen Krieg, alle, auch die Neutralen. Der Umstand, dass er nur gelegentlich, an kleinen Fronten und fast verschämt, auch militärisch aufflackert, ist kein Indiz, dass Friede wäre; das jeweils rasche und gerade vom Osten her beflissene Ersticken der verräterischen Flamme hat vornehmlich den Sinn, uns in den Glauben einzulullen, es sei nicht Krieg, sondern wirklich Friede.[6]

---

5   Karl Schmid, *Psychologische Aspekte des totalen Krieges* (Frauenfeld: 1960), p. 3.
6   Schmid, p. 14.

Schmid, without doubt one of the more sophisticated Swiss military writers, went on to argue:

> Wenn wir so üblicherweise 'totaler Krieg' sagen, denken wir an Atomangriffe, Panzerarmeen und Raketenschwärme. Aber ihr Einsatz, diese militärische Instrumentation, gehört eben gerade nicht unabdingbar zum totalen Krieg. Unabdingbar jedoch gehört es zu ihm, dass er dauernd geführt wird, unterbruchslos auf der Front der wirtschaftlichen und technischen Potentiale und pausenlos auf der Nervenfront. Wir haben schon eine entscheidende Schlacht in diesem totalen Krieg verloren, wenn wir des Glaubens sind, solange es nicht knalle, sei nicht Krieg.[7]

Military weaponry would only correspond to what was tactically called the reserve.

> So ist es im Osten logischerweise zu dem Entschlusse gekommen, die Entscheidung auf derjenigen Front zu suchen, die tatsächlich noch einen Sieg zulässt; auf der psychologischen Front winkt der Sieg durch Angst und Faszination.[8]

The consequence of this analysis is obvious: 'Der totale Krieg verlangt ein totales militärisches Denken. Total ist es, indem es keine der aussermilitärischen Fronten auslässt, weder die wirtschaftliche noch die psychologische'.[9]

The high incidence of the concept 'total' in Karl Schmid's pamphlet is by no means out of the ordinary; at the time it was a favourite word of military writers. Until the late 1960s they juxtaposed 'total war' with 'total national defence', even in official documents.[10] Because this sounded too martial in the climate created by the demands for democracy by the youth and student movements, there was a temporary switch to the more neutral formulation 'overall national defence'. Even the combination 'overall (total) national defence' can be found.[11] From about 1968 the expression

---

7   ibid., pp. 14–15.
8   ibid., p. 15.
9   ibid., p. 18.
10 'Bericht des Bundesrates an die Bundesversammlung über die Konzeption der militärischen Landesverteidigung', 6 June 1966, p. 4 and p. 18 (Bericht 66).
11 Jakob Annasohn, 'Die umfassende Landesverteidigung', in *Nichtmilitärische Landesveretidigung*. Ernst Uhlmann dargebracht (Frauenfeld: 1967), p. 21.

'General Defence', which was suited to the technocratic concepts gaining ground at the time in all areas, established itself.[12]

Leading military figures, until well on into the second half of the twentieth century, saw Switzerland endangered by war. The potential adversaries, however, gave the impression of being extremely unreal constructions. Thus Gustav Däniker, in his sensational book of 1966 *Strategie des Kleinstaats*, stated: 'Bereits 1965 ist Frankreich mit knapper Not einem kommunistischen Regime entgangen'.[13] He was referring to the reasonable success of François Mitterrand against Charles de Gaulle in the elections of December 1965. The head of the French Socialist Party remained a popular hate-figure. After his election as President in 1981, Swiss military exercise planners assumed in a 'scenario commensurate to the threat' that he had given Soviet submarines hospitality in Northern French ports and was suppressing the resulting riots amongst the local population with the help of troops from the East.[14] Gustav Däniker, who had gone on in the meantime to become a major-general and chief of staff for operational training and was thus responsible for the creation of a realistic view of the enemy, was still writing in 1982:

> Welcher militärisch interessierte und welcher besorgte Bürger hätte ihn nicht schon einmal gehabt: den Alptraum eines 'strategischen Überfalls': Eines schönen frühen Morgens landen auf allen Schweizer Flugplätzen fremde Soldaten. Panzer werden ausgeladen, fahren zu den 'strategisch' wichtigen Punkten. Unsere Behörden sind völlig überrascht.

Nonetheless he then asked: 'Hat diese Vision etwas mit Wahrscheinlichkeit oder gar mit zu erwartender Wirklichkeit zu tun?'[15] Doubtless such fears were harboured, not least by militia officers in the 1960s, and it is difficult

---

12 'Botschaft des Bundesrates an die Bundesversammlung zum Bundesgesetz über die Leitungsorganisation und den Rat für Gesamtverteidigung', 30 October 1968, in Bundesblatt 1968/II, pp. 641–84 (Botschaft Leitungsorganisation).

13 Gustav Däniker, *Strategie des Kleinstaats* (Frauenfeld: 1966), p. 167.

14 Jürg Frischknecht, 'Die Schweiz schützt sich vor Schweizern', in Hans A. Pestalozzi (ed), *Rettet die Schweiz – schafft die Armee ab* (Bern: 1982), p. 145.

15 Quoted in *Einführung in die Gesamtverteidigung*, Ausgabe II/1984 (Bern: 1984), p. 6.

to judge if they were genuine or simply a means to an end. In the mid-1960s domestic political turbulence provided the trigger – not the deeper reason – for a re-think of the concept of national defence. An intense struggle in the officer corps about the way ahead was the prelude to this. The supporters of Mobile Defence, who were close to the Zürich upper middle class, demanded increased mobility from the army by means of far-reaching mechanisation, not least by a huge increase in the air force and armoured units. More traditional officers, on the other hand, were proponents of Area Defence which was based on deeply structured prepared positions and strong infantry. They considered Mobile Defence to be unrealisable in view of the densely populated central area of Switzerland and of the high costs. However, the supporters of Mobile Defence won through in 1960 on the political level, but not without considerable cuts to the programme.[16] The very first step towards realisation, however, led up a blind alley. After a financial debacle, the so-called Mirage affair, only 57 state-of-the-art Mirage fighter planes were purchased in 1964 instead of the planned 100.[17] Thus a corner-stone of Mobile Defence collapsed.

During the Mirage affair, National Councillor Walther Bringolf, the former President of the Social-Democratic Party, demanded a re-examination of the 'Gesamtkonzeption der Landesverteidigung' by the Federal Council.[18] Discussion started on another level as well. Thus, also in 1964, Brigadier-General Charles Folletête, Head of the Department for the Territorial Service and Air Protection, presented his study 'Totale Landesverteidigung', in which he criticised deficient co-ordination between military, civilian, economic and psychological aspects of national defence.[19] On 6 June 1966 the 'Bericht des Bundesrates an die Bundesversammlung über die Konzeption der militärischen Landesverteidigung' was ready. It clearly gave greater weight to Area Defence. It referred to total national defence only in a short section in Part III on 'Hauptprobleme der nächsten

---

16 Alfred Ernst, *Die Konzeption der schweizerischen Landesverteidigung 1815 bis 1966* (Frauenfeld:1971), pp. 175–303.

17 Christian Kolbe, 'Ein "Wunderbastard" für die Obersten', in Heinz Looser et al (eds), *Die Schweiz und ihre Skandale* (Zürich: 1995), pp. 61–75.

18 Bericht 66, p. 1.

19 Hans Senn, *Friede in Unabhängigkeit* (Frauenfeld: 1983), pp. 49–50.

Planungsperiode'.[20] In his plea for the acquisition of deterrent atomic
weapons, Gustav Däniker mocked:

> Militärs aller Grade suchen heute ihren Weit- und Scharfblick zu
> beweisen, indem sie zwanzig Jahre nach Beendigung des ersten als
> solchen propagierten totalen Krieges von der Notwendigkeit sprechen,
> das Land nicht nur militärisch zu verteidigen.[21]

At the end of December 1964, the Federal Council was already charging
the departing Chief of General Staff, Jakob Annasohn, to investigate how
'eine wirksame Koordination aller Teile der totalen Landesverteidigung
herbeigeführt werden kann'.[22] Two years later he presented the Federal
Military Department, the Defence Ministry, with a detailed study in which
he – according to the synopsis of the Federal Council – proceeded on the
following assumption:

> Das Auftreten von Massenvernichtungsmitteln im totalen Krieg führt
> infolge ihrer ständig latenten Bedrohung zum Ausweichen der
> Konfliktaustragung auf die politische, wirtschaftliche, psychologische,
> elektronische und subversive Ebene. Der totale Krieg umfasst nicht nur
> die Armee, sondern das ganze Land, seine ganze Wirtschaft und vor
> allem die Zivilbevölkerung in ihrer Gesamtheit.[23]

The report of the Federal Council based on Jakob Annasohn's study split
the security policy, which was no longer called 'totale Landesverteidigung'
but 'Gesamtverteidigung', into two main areas, 'militärische Landesverteidigung' and 'zivile Landesverteidigung' which were to be based on
'geistige Landesverteidigung'. The Federal Council designated as
departments of 'zivile Landesverteidigung' foreign policy, protection of
the state, psychological national defence in the area of information
provision, civil protection, economic national defence, social safety,
protection of cultural artefacts as well as other administrative tasks
important for the war.[24] The aim in the first instance was not the creation

20 Bericht 66, p. 18 ('1. Die Eingliederung der militärischen Landesverteidigung in die
    Totale Landesverteidigung').
21 Däniker, p. 121; for contemporary criticism, compare Karl Schmid, 'Sind Atomwaffen
    für die Schweiz unerlässlich?', in *Gesammelte Werke*, vol 5 (Zürich: 1998), pp. 10–13.
22 Botschaft Leitungsorganisation, p. 641.
23 ibid., p. 642.
24 ibid., pp. 648–54.

of a new concept of security but the creation of the directing organisational structures for General Defence. The Federal Law of 27 June 1969 basically set up two bodies: the general defence Staff, consisting of representatives of the federal administration and of the army which runs parallel to and acts as a check on the Central Office for General Defence.[25] The latter started work in the spring of 1970 and developed considerable activity in penetrating, ideologically and organisationally, both state and populace with their concerns. Even before Jakob Annasohn delivered his report, high-ranking military personnel were indicating the need for detailed clarification of stategic matters.[26] The Federal Military Department acceded to the wish in May 1967 with a decree. Chief of General Staff Paul Gygli was given a 26-member 'Studienkommission für strategische Fragen' which was to work out a 'Entwurf zu einer strategischen Konzeption der Schweiz'. Under the direction of Karl Schmid, ten professors, several directors from industry and commerce, politicians and other experts set to work. In November 1969, the Commission completed its report.[27] In the first part entitled 'Staat und Strategie', it is chiefly the threats and the strategic means, i.e. the military and civilian potential, which Switzerland can muster against them which are set forth. A second part is concerned with 'besonderen Problematik der einzelnen Sektoren der Gesamtverteidigung', namely, leadership problems, the expansion of military national defence, civil protection, the preparation of a war economy and financial matters. The report was based on the notion of an 'economically self-sufficient hedgehog' which repels everything coming from outside. Gustav Däniker, who was himself a member of the Commission, noted later: 'Die Fixierung auf praktisch reine Verteidigung [...] wurde nicht nur von seinen Kritikern [...] als Mangel empfunden'.[28] Because of objections from the General Defence Staff and from Civil Protection, the publication of the report did not take place, despite the eminent membership of the Commission, until the spring of

25 *Einführung in die Gesamtverteidigung*, p. 34.
26 Senn, pp. 109–12.
27 *Grundlagen einer strategischen Konzeption der Schweiz. Bericht der Studien-kommission für stategische Fragen*, 14 November 1969 (Zürich: 1971), pp. 17–19.
28 Gustav Däniker, 'Der Einfluss der Kommission Schmid auf die Entwicklung der schweizerischen Sicherheitspolitik', in Kurt R. Spillmann, Hans Künzi (eds), *Karl Schmid als strategischer Denker* (Zürich: 1997), p. 27.

1971 and with an extremely small circulation.[29] The report achieved a slightly larger distribution only because the private foundation 'Schweizerischer Aufklärungsdienst', which subscribed to the principles of 'geistige Landesverteidigung', accepted it for its series of publications. Scarcely noticed initially, a third authority had been concerning itself since the mid-1960s with a weighty contribution to total national defence. Albert Bachmann, who as 'Colonel Bachmann' was later to exercise parliamentary commissions on several occasions, and Georges Grosjean compiled a handbook on the civilian aspects.[30] They found support from eminent professors, high-ranking military personnel, members of the National Council and other personalities; the list of those supporting the publication also includes prominent Social Democrats and not least Maurice Zermatten, President of the Swiss Writers' Union.[31] It is true that the book was produced by a private firm, but its publisher was the Federal Department of Justice and Police, the Ministry of Justice, and distributed by the 'Eidgenössische Drucksachen- und Materialzentrale', an undertaking owned by the federal administration. Every household received a copy and this required the largest book circulation ever in Switzerland. The *Zivilverteidigungsbuch* conjures up a threat which cannot be underestimated and clearly states:

> Unsere Bereitschaft muss sich auf die militärische und die zivile Landesverteidigung erstrecken und umfasst somit neben der Armee und dem Zivilschutz auch die politische, wirtschaftliche, soziale und geistige Landesverteidigung. Der umfassenden und allgegenwärtigen Bedrohung muss eine umfassende Abwehr entgegengestellt werden.[32]

There follow pages of detailed statements of extremely varying quality about the workings of civil protection should war break out, about personal precautionary measures, such as the laying-in of provisions, behaviour after atomic attacks, first aid etc. The real aim and concern is mentioned bluntly in the first half of the book:

---

29   Beat Näf, *Die konzeptionelle Entwicklung der schweizerischen Sicherheitspolitik in der Zeit iherer Entstehung 1969–1973* (Zürich: 1981), p.7
30   Albert Bachmann, Georges Grosjean, *Zivilverteidigung* (Aarau: 1969); on the various affairs centred round Bachmann, compare *Vorkommnisse im EMD. Bericht der parlamentarischen Untersuchungskommission,* (PUK EMD), 17 November 1990.
31   Bachmann, p. 4.
32   ibid, p. 30.

> Lange bevor es zu einer gewaltsamen Auseinandersetzung kommt,
> schon mitten im Frieden arbeitet der Feind unermüdlich daran,
> Misstrauen und Zwietracht zu säen, unser natürliches Selbstgefühl zu
> zerstören und unsere innere Widerstandskraft auszuhöhlen. Er tut dies
> unmerklich, in scheinbar harmloser Form getarnt, mit immer wieder-
> holten perfiden Nadelstichen, denen wir schliesslich erliegen, wenn wir
> nicht wachsam sind.[33]

There follow almost 80 pages coloured in red and yellow which purport to impress upon the readers, in descriptions which are at times extremely dubious, the conditions obtaining immediately before and during a war.

The nadir is provided by just 50 pages bearing the title 'Die zweite Form des Krieges'.[34] This is considered to be particularly dangerous, and the brief description relates openly to the end of the 1960s: 'Der Krieg ist getarnt. Er spielt sich in den äusseren Formen des Friedenszustandes ab und kleidet sich in die Gestalt einer inneren Umwälzung'.[35] The enemy sets his sights not least on 'Intellektuelle und Künstler' who are well suited to be 'Lockvögel und Aushängeschilder'.[36] He seeks to 'Parteigänger gewinnen', to 'Wehrkraft schwächen', to 'einschläfern', to 'einschüchtern' and the 'Wirtschaft schwächen'.[37] He succeeds in none of this because of the vigilance of the Swiss; administrations, trade unions, political parties and organisations see to it that suspect people do not receive top jobs. The action of the enemy is represented in an impressive organigramme.[38] At the top is the 'Zentrale der revolutionären Kriegsführung' operating on a global level and based abroad. Its 'Büro Schweiz' has 'Trupps zur Infiltration' operating by means of 'Propaganda, Spionage, Sabotage, Terror und Materialnachschub'. In addition, the Headquarters directs 'Partei-apparate für politische Kampfführung und Propaganda'. Finally, it exerts an influence on the country through 'internationale Organisationen' such as 'Friedensorganisationen, Frauen-, Jugend-, Studentenbünd usw., die auf die Zersetzung des Wehrwillens hinarbeiten'. In addition to an 'Obergrund' with legal structures, the Headquarters is creating an 'Untergrund' with

---

33   ibid, p. 145.
34   ibid, pp. 225–72.
35   ibid, p. 227.
36   ibid, p. 228.
37   ibid, p. 248.
38   ibid, pp. 246–47.

'vorbereiteten Zellen in Behörden, Verwaltungen, Verkehrsbetrieben, Presse, Radio, Fernsehen usw'. It is also surprising how the enemy seeks to break the will of the victim, especially as Ernst Wüthrich, the President of the Swiss Trades' Union Congress, acted to promote the *Zivilverteidigungsbuch*: it begins with a strike in the metal industry, followed by a demonstration by textile workers, the election of a new leadership for the metal workers' union and strikes in public transport.[39]

So that it was clear that they were not intending to write fiction, the authors stated: 'Die zweite Form des Krieges, so wie sie jetzt geschildert wurde, ist Gegenwart. Solches geschieht täglich um uns und unter uns'.[40] This virulent campaign conducted under the aegis of the Minister of Justice provoked anger amongst critical intellectuals as well as amongst the youthful activists in the new social movements. Against them, however, were ranged practically the entire political elite, stretching well into the Social Democratic Party. A rupture ensued in the Swiss Writers' Union. The President, Maurice Zermatten, had prepared the French edition of the *Zivilverteidigungsbuch* and had made certain formulations more pointed. For example, he expressly called writers and critical intellectuals preferred helpers of the enemy. After the Committee had supported Zermatten, Friedrich Dürrenmatt, Max Frisch and the majority of the rising younger generation resigned. Most of them came together later in the 'Gruppe Olten' which from then on played a much more important role in the Swiss literary scene.[41]

The struggle for a concept of total or General Defence came to a close with a report on security policy.[42] Even before the public knew of the principles established by the Schmid Commission, the Federal Council had in September 1970 charged the Central Office for General Defence with working them up into a strategy capable of being translated into a policy with a 'doktrinärem Charakter'.[43] During this process, the main title changed from 'Konzeption der Gesamtverteidigung' to 'Sicherheits-

---

39   ibid, p. 252.
40   ibid, p. 248.
41   *Literatur geht nach Brot. Die Geschichte des Schweizerischen Schriftsteller-verbandes*, pp. 92–5 and pp. 153–87.
42   'Bericht des Bundesrates an die Bundesversammlung über die Sicherheitspolitik der Schweiz' (Konzeption der Gesmatverteidigung), 27 June 1971 (Bericht 73).
43   Senn, p. 132.

politik der Schweiz', not least because the Social Democratic Party could be more firmly tied in with this less incriminating title.[44] In 1973/4 the report was laid before Parliament which noted its contents positively; in the National Council, the determined critics managed to achieve five votes.[45]

Like its predecessors, the report started from a sombre assessment of the situation: 'Die innere Lage selbst europäischer Staaten ist durch widerrechtliche Handlungen und Umsturzversuche gekennzeichnet'.[46] A section on security aims follows, contained in the formula 'Friede in Unabhängigkeit'. Then the threat on four levels of conflict is mentioned: 'Zustand relativen Friedens', 'Indirekte Kriegsführung', 'Konventioneller Krieg', and 'Krieg mit Massenvernichtungsmitteln'.[47] The latter two, since they are neither topical nor probable, are mentioned only briefly. Relative peace is held to be unstable and serves 'Mächten' which are not further defined to 'durch politischen, wirtschaftlichen und propagandistisch-psychologischen Druck ihre Einflusssphären zu vergrössern'. The description becomes particularly plastic with indirect warfare which is growing in significance:

> Ihre Urheber, ob sie zugunsten eines fremden Staates, im Banne einer fremden Ideologie oder aus anarchistischen Motiven handeln, nützen innerstaatliche Gegensätze und alle Formen des politischen oder gesellschaftlichen Unbehagens von Bevölkerungsgruppen für ihre Zwecke aus. Sie arbeiten durch Verunglimpfung, Einschüchterung und Gewalt auf die Lähmung der staatlichen Organe und der demokratischen Willensbildung hin und streben die Auflösung der freiheitlichen Ordnung an, was ihnen die Verwirklichung ihrer Ziele gestatten soll.[48]

For improved co-ordination, binding situation assessments, the so-called 'strategischen Fälle', are fixed for all authorities involved. They range from 'Normalfall=Zustand des relativen Friedens' to 'Besetzungsfall =Besetzung von Landesteilen', and in between is the civilian orientated

---

44 Näf, p. 11; compare also Sozialdemokratische Partei der Schweiz, *Das Leitbild für eine friedensstrategische Sicherheitspolitik unseres Landes*, 30 September/1 October 1972.

45 Ulrich Zwygart, *Die Gesamtverteidigungskonzeption unter besonderer Berücksichtigung der strategischen Fälle* (Diessenhofen: 1983), pp. 10–22.

46 Bericht 73, p. 3.

47 ibid, pp. 8–10.

48 ibid, p. 9.

'Katastrophenfall=Grosse Schadenereignisse'.[49] There follow statements about the main strategic tasks of self-preservation, securing peace, crisis management and prevention of war or, in the worst scenario, waging war, damage control and resistance in occupied areas. The fifth section, by far the longest, deals with the 'strategischen Mittel', split into military and civilian. The latter comprise civil protection, economic provision for war, information, psychological resistance and protection of the state. To this is added the co-ordination of services in the sectors of communication, ambulance services, protection against atomic and chemical attack, veterinary services, supplies and transport as well as administrative tasks important for the war. Finally, there had to be an appropriate leadership structure. The report offered sufficient starting-points to tie the entire institutions of society into General Defence – the phrase 'security policy' was not able to establish itself at this point – , attempts to do this occurred frequently until well into the 1980s.[50] An expansion of the area of responsibility to include natural and industrial catastrophes served as a justification for this. Thus plans were created to organise the populace largely along the lines of a model which can be imagined as five concentric circles. In the centre there is a small unit of professional soldiers. The second circle is formed by those liable for military service who are deployed as far as possible in accordance with their professional skills. Round them are grouped the Civil Protection, consisting of men who are either not or no longer in the army. Specific professional duties, performed mainly by women in so-called co-ordinated services, that is, the medical corps, the veterinary service, protection of cultural artefacts, supply services or pastoral care form the fourth circle. To the fifth were assigned those not yet accounted for, mainly women and children, without, however, any precise specifications as to their function. The cantons equipped themselves with catastrophe laws which enabled recourse to the services of further sections of the populace. One weak point was never eradicated however, since the inclusion of women was only marginally successful.

---

49   ibid, p. 13
50   For what follows, compare Peter Hug, 'Von der Risikoakkumulation zur Notstands-
      gesellschaft', *Widerspruch*, 14 (1987), pp. 8–22; Peter Hug, 'Die allgemeine
      Dienstpflicht', in *Handbuch Frieden Schweiz* (Basel: 1986), pp. 123–53; Peter Hug,
      'Mit dem Zivilschutz zur Notstandsgesellschaft', in *Schutzraum Schweiz* (Bern:
      1988), pp. 111–97.

In addition to these plans, which for the most part could only be partially realised, the notion that total defence was necessary inspired further interventions in civilian life. A Parliamentary Commission of Enquiry discovered in 1989 that the federal police had collected together more than 820,000 people, firms and organisations in their files. An analysis of the years 1931 to 1990 showed that surveillance increased massively after 1966. Thus well over half of all the files had been compiled in the years 1966 to 1985, that is to say, at the time when General Defence was flourishing.[51] Appearance in the files could have serious disadvantages when those concerned were seeking employment, and could even lead to professional exclusion from public service. Anti-military activities directed against the presence of the army in civilian society – extraordinary by the standards of Western Europe – were also pursued with great zeal. Usually, it was to do with political expressions of opinion and with refusal to do military service.[52] A particular sensation was caused by the legal dispute between 1970 and 1973 about the publication in a young people's magazine of a slightly amended version of a text by Wolfgang Borchert, 'Sag Nein!' It went as far as the Federal Court and ended with a judgement against the editors 'wegen Aufforderung zur Verletzung militärischer Dienst-pflichten'.[53] As an example of cultural General Defence, the so-called 'Haarbefehl' may be mentioned.[54] In the course of the 1960s, the clothing and hair-styles of the younger generation became increasingly different from those of the older generation.[55] Long-haired men caused particular displeasure to traditionalists. A solution was found for those of them who were fit for military service. Because, up to the age of 50, they had to do 13 spells of military service, they could be ordered, under threat of sanctions, to have the same number of short haircuts, an infringement of rights usual in few dictatorships.[56]

51   Georg Kreis (ed), *Staatsschutz in der Schweiz* (Bern: 1993), p. 45.
52   Max Schmid, *Demokratie von Fall zu Fall* (Zürich: 1976), pp. 334–420.
53   Ibid, pp. 373–74.
54   *Schweizerische Armee, Dienstreglement* (DR 67), new edition 1971, p.103.
55   Bernard Degen, 'Italiener, Spanier, Griechen, "junge Mädchen in Miniröcken" und "langhaarige Jünglinge"', in Bernard Degen (ed), *Fenster zur Geschichte* (Basel: 1992), pp. 307–23.
56   Schmid, pp. 381–82.

It is certainly not wrong to see in the rise of total national defence a basic change in the scenario of threat as well. More and more people looked upon the external enemy, whom they wished to keep at bay with tanks, fighter aircraft or even atomic bombs, as a decreasing danger. It was not simply the military who sought to fill the gap arising in the threat scenario with an inner enemy whom they could drive into a corner with national security measures and military justice. Similar considerations are to be found in other countries as well, albeit not under nearly as much military influence. One recalls the emergency laws passed to massive public protest in 1968 in the Federal Republic of Germany.

Increased threat seemed for many to be heralded by profound economic, political, social and cultural changes from the mid-1960s at the latest. Effects were obvious in the most private sphere, in the family, since the number of divorces, which had changed very little since the Second World War, suddenly rose considerably.[57] In the eyes of many what could be seen in the streets changed alarmingly too since the booming economy attracted masses of foreign workers, mainly Italians. This fostered the notion of 'Überfremdung'.[58] Culturally, too, the country was in the opinion of many moving towards the abyss. It is true that music programmes on Swiss radio and television remained extremely traditional for a long time. But Anglo-American rock stars, through foreign radio and television stations, records and audio-cassettes, early on had undivided attention, mainly with urban youth. In literature, Max Frisch and Friedrich Dürrenmatt, who had long since gone beyond the limits of Swiss creative writing, were joined by a generation of critical writers.[59] On the political level, with the xenophobic organisations on the right and the new social movements on the left, forces appeared which placed the consensus of the governing parties under strain. Not a few German-Swiss saw separatism, which was striving for the separation of the Jura from the Canton of Bern, as an inadmissible demand. Finally, there arose in the narrower area of the army an increasingly disturbing problem in addition to the short-lived

57   *Historische Statistik der Schweiz* (Zürich: 1996), p. 205.
58   For contemporary criticism, compare Max Frisch, 'Überfremdung 1', in *Max Frisch. Schweiz als Heimat?* (Frankfurt am Main: 1990), pp. 219–21 [1965], and 'Überfremdung 2', pp. 223–44 [1966].
59   Klaus Pezold et al, *Geschichte der deutschsprachigen Schweizer Literatur im 20. Jahrhundert* (Berlin: 1991), pp. 167–214.

Mirage affair. Because Switzerland was the last European democracy to offer those who refused to do military service a civilian alternative, these people were until the beginning of the 1990s judged by military courts. From 1963 the number increased considerably, and numerous trials undermined the reputation of military justice in lasting fashion.[60]

The restricted world of *geistige Landesverteidigung*, in which many had comfortably installed themselves, was relentlessly crumbling. It was obvious that this should be attributed to an external enemy. It is true that the popular East-West pattern was, with the escalation of the Vietnam war, beginning to lose its persuasiveness, in urban centres to begin with. Yet the notions developed in the *Zivilverteidigungsbuch* still had a considerable following, in particular that of a 'Zentrale der revolutionären Kriegsführung'. The site of this is never mentioned in official documents for considerations of political neutrality; but everyone knew that Moscow was meant. In this direction an impressive defence system was erected – a gigantic strategic error. It should have been clear to attentive observers at the time that the consumer society in the United States, Hollywood and Anglo-American rock stars were undermining the society of *geistige Landesverteidigung* far more effectively than the old gentlemen in the Kremlin. When the National Council approved the concept of General Defence in June 1974 without any great controversy, the well-known columnist Oskar Reck commented: 'Das Sicherheitskonzept als solches bewirkt einen rhetorischen Schulterschluss, wie man ihn auf diesem Gebiete sonst nur im Zustand nationaler Bedrohung erlebt'.[61] One thinks spontaneously of the Second World War which for decades occupied a central position in Swiss self-perception. Thus, as late as 1989, the Federal Military Department invited, under the rubric 'Diamond', veterans of the years 1939 to 1945 from the entire country to regional meetings.[62] In assembly halls and marquees the mobilisation of the late summer of 1939 was celebrated with speeches, meals popular in wartime, alcohol and occasionally with

---

60 Karl W. Haltiner, *Milizarmee – Bürgerleitbild oder angeschlagenes Ideal* (Frauenfeld: 1985), p. 310; Schmid, pp. 390–402.
61 *Basler Nachrichten*, 15 June 1974.
62 On this compare Simone Chiquet, 'Der Anfang einer Auseinandersetzung', in *Studien und Quellen. Zeitschrift des Schweizerischen Bundesarchivs*, no. 24 (Bern: 1998), pp. 193–227; the title 'Diamond' is a metaphor from Gottfried Keller's poem 'Eidgenossenschaft'.

additional attractions. When the fiftieth anniversary of the German capitulation was marked in May 1995 in the rest of Europe, there was a remarkable reticence in Switzerland. This ought not to be surprising for in 1945 the end of the War caused considerable embarrassment to official Switzerland.[63] It was not until the mid-1990s, with the international debate about the role of the Swiss banks, that the positive evaluation of the war period was permanently shattered.

Wartime society developed its formative power over a considerable section of the populace for a variety of reasons. In contrast to almost all other European countries, Switzerland was not involved in hostilities. It is true that ruptured lines of supply created difficulties, and the period of military service, on average somewhat more than two years, placed considerable strain on those liable for military service and on their families. And it was not always possible to suppress fear. On the other hand, there were starting-points for a positive assessment. The economic recession was limited, so that the relative position vis-a-vis states caught up in the War improved markedly. The widespread unemployment, which had persisted until the end of the 1930s, largely disappeared, and social tensions between capital and labour did not acquire a certain intensity again until towards the end of the War. The in part extremely heated political controversies of the previous decade went into abeyance, even if the Social Democratic Party did not receive a seat in the federal government until the end of 1943. Moreover, a considerable cultural rapprochement took place within the framework of *geistige Landesverteidigung*. Finally, the absence of an enemy invasion led to approval of the army the like of which had never been known. Significantly, it was not, as in other democracies, a political leader who incorporated the will to resist, but the Commander-in-Chief, General Henri Guisan.[64] The image of the self-sufficient hedgehog, whose quills stop potential attackers, enjoyed uninterrupted popularity until the end of the 1980s. Then even military planners came to the conclusion that it can 'nicht mehr Leitbild unseres Sicherheits-

---

63   Mario König, '"Jetzt, wo der Krieg zu Ende ist..."', in Erich Gysling, Mario König, Michael T. Ganz, *1945–Die Schweiz im Friedensjahr* (Zürich: 1995), pp. 88–101.
64   On the extraordinary personality cult round General Guisan in the post-war era, see Willi Gautschi, *General Henri Guisan* (Zürich: 1989), pp. 734–58.
65   Däniker, 'Einfluss der Kommission Schmid', p. 27.

denkens'.[65] Negative aspects have faded in the course of the years. The notion of a community holding its own in a hostile environment by setting aside its social and political difficulties acted for decades as a reservoir for arguments against attempts at reform.

The vision of a total defence society offered even soldiers with a considerably odd view of the world a framework for unusual forms of self-realisation.[66] Thus different authorities within the Federal Military Department collected data on suspicious persons and on so-called enemies of the army and did not hesitate to work with civilian or even private offices in the course of their snooping. Additionally, the so-called secret services caused a sensation. There was for example the project, which became known as the 'Secret Army' or 'P–26' of a 'Kaderorganisation für die Vorbereitung des Widerstandes im feindbesetzten Gebiet', which comprised 400 people.[67] Then there was the extraordinary intelligence service which exposed itself to international ridicule when Austrian soldiers caught one of its agents at the end of 1979.[68] It was not until the winter of 1989/90 when a section of the press fiercely criticised the organisations operating outwith parliamentary control that they were in part disbanded.

In the 1990s the supporters of General Defence were forced increasingly onto the defensive. They themselves saw the reason mainly in the great changes in Eastern Europe.[69] The result of the referendum on the initiative 'Für eine Schweiz ohne Armee' was also a severe blow. Over a third of those voting opted for the abolition of the army, amongst young voters there was even a clear majority for this.[70] More profound developments had a more lasting effect, however. The increasing internationalisation of the economy, not least the penetration of the top echelons of Swiss firms by foreign managers, created a gap between the economic and the military elite. In civilian life, values, which are considered necessary for its functioning by the army, lost their significance in favour of those such as individual autonomy, establishment of personal identity, development of the personality or participation which all undermine the military

---

66   See PUK EMD.
67   PKU EMD, p. 197 and p. 202.
68   PUK EMD, p. 187 and p. 240.
69   Laurent François Carrel (ed), *Schweizer Armee heute und in Zukunft* (Thun: 1996), p. 18.
70   *Année politique suisse. Schweizerische Politik 1989* (Bern: 1990), pp. 82–5.

concept of discipline.[71] Economists highlighted the extremely extravagant use of personnel in the army and in Civil Protection.[72] The burgeoning bureaucracy of General Defence was difficult to square with business management notions of units responding rapidly and flexibly. Thus even the former director of the federal military administration came to the conclusion:

> Eine für die Ausschöpfung aller Ressourcen strukturierte totale Landesverteidigung (später beschönigend 'Gesamtverteidigung' genannt) hat sich im Laufe von Jahrzehnten einen eigentlichen Speckgürtel umgelegt. [...] Dieses schwerfällige Instrumentarium kann bekanntlich nur mit einem staatspolitischen Kraftakt einsatzbereit gemacht werden, was sich unter den heutigen aussenpolitischen Vernetzungen kaum mehr jemals praktisch vorstellen lässt.[73]

At the end of 1998 the Federal Council abolished the Central Office for General Defence, once the focus of great expectations, by means of a simple decree.[74]

The vision of General Defence, backward-looking despite modern features, left deep traces. The programme of permanent preparation for war, fortunately only partly realisable, drastically limited diversity of opinion by seeking to smear divergent positions as un-Swiss. When the majority of the political elite finally brought themselves to accept integration into the UN and into the European Union, the conservative and extreme Right opposition brought down the necessary parliamentary resolutions, not least by arguments reinforced by General Defence. Additionally there is a continuing tendency, with problems of the most diverse kind, to think first of a military deployment. Whether it is policing duties such as guarding foreign embassies, additional duties for the customs service or increased surveillance of national frontiers, a social service such as the care of refugees or clearing up after a storm – the call always goes

---

71   Karl W. Haltiner, 'Das Militär im Wandel der Wertvorstellungen', in Carrel, p. 445.
72   Thomas Straubhaar, Michael Schleicher (eds), *Wehrpflicht oder Berufsarmee?* (Bern: 1996).
73   Hans-Ulrich Ernst, 'Change-Management in der Sicherheitspolitik', *Neue Zürcher Zeitung*, no. 82, 10/11 April 1999.
74   'Verordnung über die Aufhebung der Zentralstelle für Gesamtverteidigung', 25 November 1998, in *Amtliche Sammlung des Bundesrechts*, 1999, pp. 915–16.

out for the army. But arguably the worst effects have come from the fact that, at a time when in most democratic states plans for re-orientation were under discussion, in large sections of Swiss society the talk was still only of defence.

Translated by Malcolm Pender

ARMIN KÜHNE

When Citizens become Customers: Institutional Conditions for the Democratic Accountability of New Public Management in a Direct Democracy

Reception and Perception of NPM in Switzerland

For the 'results-oriented public management',[1] as New Public Management (NPM) is called in Switzerland, the time seemed ripe. In the 1990s the publications had an astonishing effect on practice in administrative structures which has scarcely encountered any other concept in the field of economics in recent years.[2] In Switzerland, as in other countries, a demand arose for reform in local councils and then in cantons.[3] Overnight, as it were, a discussion on the theoretical and political aspects of administration was forming a focus for interested experts. A rash of conferences quickly disseminated the new ideas. The spread of what were originally economic perspectives to social and legal problems happened with incredible speed. Today NPM is at a political threshold of its reception

---

1   E. Buschor, 'Wirkungsorientierte Verwaltungsführung'. Wirtschaftliche Publikationen, *Zürcher Handelskammer*, Heft 32 (1993).

2   E. Buschor and K. Schedler (eds), 'Perspectives on Performance Measurement and Public Sector Accounting', *Schriftenreiche Finanzirtschaft und Finanzrecht*, no. 71 (Bern/Stuttgart/Vienna:1994), E. Buschor, 'Das Konzept des New Public Management', *Schweizer Arbeitgeber*, 6 (1995), 272–76. K. Schedler, *Ansätze einer wirkungsorientierten Verwaltungführung. Von der Idee des New Public Management zum konkreten Gestaltungsmodell. Fallbeispiel Schweiz* (Bern: 1995), P. Hablützel, T. Haldemann, K. Schedler, K. Schwaar (eds), *Umbruch in Politik und Verwaltung. Ansichten und Erfahrungen zum New Public Management in der Schweiz* (Bern: 1995).

3   For an overview see K. Schedler, 'The State of Public Management Reforms in Switzerland', in W. Kickert (ed), *Public Management and Administrative Reform in Western Europe* (London: 1998), pp. 121–140.

in respect of parliaments, and so is at its politically most necessary but also most difficult stage to date.

NPM was from the outset not a coherent package of theories, but an amalgam of existing ideas for reform which were put together with NPM into a common discourse. The central elements of NPM are:

– an increased focus on the output of public administrations so as to direct administration, hitherto operating in accordance with the law of conditions, towards its final goal;

– a new theory of steering which, on the basis of a clear distinction between policy and administration or 'strategic' and 'operative steering', aimed at giving greater autonomy to decentralised administrative units so that they accord with the new demands made by social and economic developments for flexibility, speed, economic rationality, quality and transparency;

– the central legitimation was now expressed in the new 'orientation towards the customer';

– performance agreements and globalised budgets used by contract management were selected as the main instruments of control for the quasi-autonomous agencies.

The following factors contributed to the speedy introduction of NPM reforms in Switzerland:

– a generation of leaders coming forward in admininistrations, consultancies and academic life pushing for professionalisation, which is linked to NPM;

– (neo)-liberal and social democratic circles are adopting the reform proposals. From the (neo)-liberal point of view, there is hope of realising long-standing demands for making the state 'leaner' and for increasing governance (especially as regards time and money). From the social democratic point of view, the social and welfare state, a project suffering from efficiency deficits because of new social problems and needs, is to receive a more complex steering on a new level and be given new life.[4]

– the major significance up until now in Switzerland of the third sector won fresh recognition for social governance of political areas by private

---

4   See for example H. Willke, *Systemtheorie III: Steuerungstheorie. Grundzüge einer Theorie der Steuerung komplexer Sozialsysteme* (Stuttgart: 1995).

and mixed economic organisations.[5] From this perspective, the setting up of agencies by NPM is regarded as an adequate strategy for giving direction to a very heterogenous and increasingly fragmented civil society. The hope for reinforcement of autonomous claims for steering from non-state players[6] conflicts nevertheless with the uncertainties accompanying NPM in respect of reduction and re-distribution of state services. What is new is that subventions are dependent on their efficiency and effectiveness and are being checked against this for the first time.[7]

– the scarcity of state financial resources makes the need for reform more pressing and so supports the NPM strategies of out-sourcing and decentralising state services. This scarcity is also the source of fears that, with NPM, competitive and wealthy social classes (the new 'customers'?) would win support in conflicts about distribution. Additionally, fears about jobs and work-related stress are reinforced by NPM. Expert circles are divided as to whether NPM is necessary because of the shortage of financial resources (this tends to be the view of opponents) or is independent of this circumstance (this tends to be the view of proponents). For the latter, the shortage of resources coincides simply by chance with the reform which is being driven by altogether different motives, motives deriving from a basic need for reform of political-social governance[8] or institutional steering and control.[9]

Because of all these factors NPM developed fast. Equally quickly, a critical attitude towards NPM arose to shape state services more efficiently and more economically not simply from the point of view of the customers and taxpayers. Efficiency in state measures going beyond that is being

5   M. Finger, B. Ruchat (eds), *Pour une Nouvelle Approche du Management Public. Réflexions autour de Michel Crozier* (Paris: 1997); S. Catttacin, I. Kissling-Näf, 'Subsidiäres Staatshandeln', *Schweizerische Zeitschrift für politische Wissenschaft*, 3 (1997), no. 3, Sonderheft.

6   P. Mastronardi/ K. Schedler, *New Public Management in Staat und Recht. Ein Diskurs* (Bern: 1988), p. 6.

7   *Bericht des Bundesrates über die Prüfung der Bundessubventionen*, 25 June 1997.

8   R. Mayntz, 'L'administration publique dans le changement societal', in Finger/ Ruchat, *Pour une Nouvelle Approche du Management Public*, pp. 97–111.

9   U. Klöti, 'Switzerland', in D.C.Rowat (ed), *Public Administration in Developed Democracies* (New York/Basel: 1988).

demanded.[10] The openness of NPM to such demands has united its critics and proponents up until now in a broad coalition for reform. At the risk of endangering this coalition, NPM can only limit itself to lowering business costs and eliminating state deficits.

Institutional Reforms as a Condition for NPM

The steering in many areas of policy today is characterised by conflicting goals and the use of uncertain resources,[11] it is influenced by networks of multi-national players outwith bureaucratic control,[12] and is to this extent dependent on a high measure of political consultation (in the sense of governance).[13] Deficits in policy management cannot be compensated for by management concepts, however modern, if they are economically restricted.[14] For this reason, NPM has been moved into the arena of more comprehensive reforms of the political system.[15] In the interim, comprehensive reforms of government, administration and leadership of the state have come to be regarded as the condition for a lasting NPM. In the debate, it is therefore mainly in the following areas that institutional reforms of the political system, which go beyond economic beginnings, are being encouraged.

10   P. Knöpfel, 'Plädoyer für ein tatsächlich wirkungsorientiertes Public Management', *Schweizerische Zeitschrift für politische Wissenschaft*, 2 (1996), no. 1, pp. 151–67.
11   J. D. Thompson/ A. Tuden, 'Strategies, structures and processes of organizational decision', in J. D. Thompson (ed), *Comparative Studies in Administration* (Pittsburgh: 1959); M. D. Cohen/ J. G. March/ J. P. Olsen, 'A garbage-can model of organisational choice', *Administrative Science Quarterly*, no. 17, 1972, pp. 1–25.
12   S. Kickert, *Public Governance in the Netherlands. An Alternative to Anglo-American Managerialism*, 1995; Mayntz, op.cit.
13   W. Kickert (ed), *Public Management and Administrative Reform in Western Europe* (London: 1998).
14   Knöpfel, op. cit.
15   S. Hug/ P. Sciarini (eds), 'Staatsreform', *Schweizerische Zeitschrift für politische Wissenschaft,* Sonderheft, 2 (1996).

De-regulation and Contracting Out of Administrative Units within the Framework of the Guarantor State and Civil Society

The political core of NPM is formed by endeavours to contract out and decentralise public services (agency building)[16] in order to increase the flexibility of administrative units of action vis-a-vis recipients and customers as well as to aim for a greater competitiveness amongst public services. At the federal level, the '4 circles model' of state management was developed, which intends to make possible a step-by-step realisation of these aims in certain areas of administration.[17] The basic theory of management behind this requires a difference to be made between centrally strategic and decentralised operative leadership, between management and supervision.[18] In the centre, corresponding endeavours are supported by an examination of the tasks of the state.[19] The 'product definitions' based on this and the re-modelling of the production process form the core of the NPM administration projects.

Customer-oriented 'product portfolios' draw criticism from public officials if the new customer orientation seeks to displace the cultural values of a public service traditionally oriented towards citizens. Moreover, the customer orientation which legitimises NPM has not convinced large sections of public employees and experts that freedoms deriving from

---

16 RVOG Art. 44 ('Regierungs- und Verwaltungsorganisationsgesetz', 21 March 1997), *Systematische Rechtssammlung des Bundes*, SR 172.010.

17 Schweizerische Bundeskanzlei, 'Regierungs- und Verwaltungsreform. Projektstand – Resultate Screening – Weiteres Vorgehen', *Bericht an den Bundesrat*, 11 February 1998, p. 18.

18 'New Public Management. Ein neues Konzept für die Verwaltung des Bundes?', in *Schriftenreihe des Eidgenössischen Personalamtes*, vol 1 (Bern: 1995).

19 Verwaltungskontrolle des Bundesrates, 'Überprüfung der Bundesaufgaben', *Bericht an den Bundesrat*, 20 February 1995; Verwaltungskontrolle des Bundesrates, 'Leitfaden der VKB für die systematische und periodische Überprüfung der wesentlichen Aufgaben (ÜBA)', 1996; Regierungsrat des Kantons Zürich, 'Bericht zur Aufgaben- und Leistungsüberprüfung', 9 September 1998; Sachverständigenrat, 'Schlanker Staat. Leitfaden zur Modernisierung von Behörden. Abschlussbericht', vol 3 (Bonn: 1998); G. Schmid, 'Überlegungen zur Auslese von Staatsaufgaben im politischen System der Schweiz', *ASSP*, 30 (1990), pp. 121–35.

decentralisation and contracting out offer protection against errors in existing policy management which is in any case fragmented and incoherent[20] and against an unequal distribution of public goods and services according to the yardstick of the legality principle.[21]

An attempt is currently in train to overcome this criticism from administrative personnel and experts by legal considerations relating to administration[22] and government with the intention of reconciling the legality of government action and the traditional values of the public service with the NPM strategy of decentralisation and granting independence to administrative units. The proposed guarantor state[23] limits itself to the definition of goals and their realisation by non-state players. This follows on from the existing legitimacy of subsidiary delivery of goals by social organisations well established in Switzerland in the tertiary sector.[24] In this way, suspicions of a neo-liberal dismantling of the state are to be allayed so as to make possible the compromise necessary for a reform coalition between supporters and opponents of deregulation, contracting out and decentralisation. Services are not to be dismantled but organised afresh. The state is to withdraw from certain areas in which it fulfills tasks on its own and instead delegate them by means of financial support (subventions), legal support (procedural rules) and organisational support (technical support).

The political difficulties in practice, the conflicts accompanying these processes, however, in addition to differences of principle between supporters and opponents of privatisation, again and again display aspects of the unresolved question about the extent to which the improved customer services (including the administrative gains in efficiency) unjustifiably create disadvantaged groups (for example, the old, the poor, the uneducated,

---

20   OECD, *In Search of Results. Performance Management Practices* (Paris: 1997).
21   Mastronardi/ Schedler, pp. 72–80.
22   D. Berchtold/ A. Hofmeister (eds), 'Die öffentliche Verwaltung im Spannungsfeld zwischen Legalität und Funktionsfähigkeit. Schnittstellen Verwaltungsrecht und Verwaltungsmanagement', *Schriftenreihe der Schweiz. Gesellschaft für Verwaltungswissenschaften*, vol 30 (Bern: 1995).
23   Mastronardi/ Schedler, op. cit. The concept of the 'guarantor state' refers in German to the 'Gewährleistungsstaat'. Compared to other translations such as 'enabling and granting state' or 'responsible state' the term 'guarantor state' is preferred here.
24   S. Cattacin/ I. Kissling-Näf, op. cit.

the immobile, the unemployed, and others) who, because of their circumstances, cannot make use of the services on offer.

Improvement of Governance by Government Reform

Since the beginning of the 1990s, that is to say before the high point of NPM, the endeavours of the Federation to re-structure its institutional assumptions were increased[25] with a view to improving the management capability (decision-making ability) of the government and of the entire system. After the government suffered a defeat in the 1996 referendum on the new RVOG (Government and Public Administration Organisation Bill), it was possible to distinguish two trends. On the one hand, reform of government was increasingly linked to elements of NPM, whose career had just begun. Thus the existing need for reform could be given new impetus. On the other hand, however, the reform of government was simultaneously limited to an administrative reform which cannot fulfill the essential postulates of an increase in the ability of the Federal Council to manage. Central postulates of NPM have since then been successfully aimed at by the Government and Administration Reform (RVR).[26]

As with previous attempts,[27] a reform of government has not succeeded. The introduction of state secretaries, which were to have unburdened the government from administrative functions and to have contributed to a strengthening of its strategic and political management functions, was rejected in the referendum of 1996. Instead, the government reform was put back until the planned reform of governance[28] in which the relationship between government and parliament is to be re-shaped.

---

25   AGFB (Arbeitsgruppe Führungsstrukturen des Bundes), *Zwischenbericht über Abklärungen betreffend die Führungsstrukturen des Bundes: Notwendigkeit und Kriterien einer Regierungsreform, Modelle des Regierungssystems*, 23 November 1991.
26   Bundesrat, *Bericht des Bundesrates über seine Geschäftsführung* (Bern: 1999).
27   U. Klöti, 'Regierungsreform in der Schweiz: ein langweriger Prozess', in *Kleinstaat und Menschenrechte. Festgabe für Gerard Batliner zum 65. Geburtstag* (Basel/Frankfurt: 1993), pp. 495–513.
28   *Jahresplanung des Bundesrates*, 1997.

Up until now, because the reform has been limited to an administrative 'internal modernisation', the citizen has not seen very much of all these efforts nor has he/she supported them. The defeat of the government in the referendum of 1996[29] was supported by populist circles who are still today rejecting the reform as technocratic. That voters were not convinced by the reform is, however, due to the attitude of the government which was not convinced about a better disposition of strategic and operative administrative functions in its areas and, instead, feared loss of power in shedding administrative functions.

NPM and Citizens in a Direct Democracy

Strengthening the role of the citizen in a direct democracy demands participation from citizens in the sense of being involved in planning and being affected by the conseqences of NPM projects. The concept of the 'guarantor state' (fulfillment of functions through intermediary organisations from the tertiary sector), socially oriented and propagated by proponents of NPM, in no way runs counter to this aim, but does not actively expand it either by means of new forms of participation within the framework of the 'activating state'.[30] The predominant concept of the customer is not oriented towards the citizen but towards the consumer.[31] Moreover, the tight financial situation of the state considerably restricts its room for manoeuvre as a guarantor. Socially oriented citizens can easily become competitors for scarce subventions. Which groups of customers under conditions of intensified selection are to be served by administrative units governed by NPM is a question which will scarcely be able to be

---

29   S. Hug et al, 'Analyse der eidgenössischen Abstimmung vom Juni 1996', *Vox*, no. 59, 1996.
30   J-D. Delley, 'New Public Management und neue staatliche Herausforderungen', in P. Hablützel et al, *Umbruch in Politik und Verwaltung*, pp. 439–51; S. von Bandemer/ B. Blanke/ J. Hilbert, 'Staatsaufgaben – Von der "schleichenden Privatisierung" zum "aktivierenden Staat"', in F. Behrens et al (eds), *Den Staat neu denken. Reformperspektiven für die Landesverwaltungen* (Berlin: 1995), pp. 41–61.
31   Representative of this is R. Koppel: 'NPM. Kundinnen- und Bürgerorientierung von Verwaltungen', P. Hablützel et al, *Umbruch in Politik und Verwaltung*, pp. 337–59.

answered by managers alone. NPM cannot prevent its aims for customer-directed and competitive administration becoming a political matter in conditions of financial limitation, to the chagrin of those who have a narrow economic view of the world.

From the perspective of participatory, socially oriented requirements society does not simply demand high quality in public services but, as a measure of its freedoms and its momentum, also social opportunities for the realisation of central values such as engagement and participation in relation to government institutions. From this perspective, NPM projects will have to create their legitimacy increasingly by the participation of the citizens in shaping the supply of public services.

The direct democratic system makes resources available to answer such political challenges with its own means. Performance agreements and globalised budgets for private organisations involved in the fulfillment of state functions can, for example, be put before the people in a referendum. Thus the Canton of Bern, suffering severely from financial problems, put to the people for their decision (referendum of 29 November 1998) its subventions and its corresponding commissioning of a public utility undertaking (Vereinigung für Beratung, Integrationshilfe und Gemein-wesenarbeit).

It is true that putting individual projects to the traditional decision-making processes of direct democracy does not constitute an expansion of citizens' participation. Nonetheless, the value of such direct democratic decisions lies precisely in heading off the uncertainties caused in the electorate by the intensified competition for public resources. NPM can gain legitmacy with the help of direct democracy because it can employ the (plebiscitary) 'customer questionnaires' available institutionally in this form as a basis for decisions. A new form of participation is not of course developed in this way.

Abroad, especially at council level, initiatives are apparent of an NPM oriented towards the citizen which produces forms of participation which offer the citizen, as someone affected by policies, the opportunity for input.[32] It is true that new forms of participation are visible in Switzerland (for

32 P. De Leon, 'Administrative Reform and Democratic Accountability', in Kickert, *Public Management and Administrative Reform*, pp. 233–51.

example, public forums in the areas of waste disposal or gene technology), but which are not copied by NPM. Against that, direct democratic initiatives can be observed in OECD countries which go beyond the creation of an acceptance of 'consumerist managerialism'[33] and which permit citizens to participate in NPM programmes in the form of partnership planning models (citizen-quality-feedback-systems). In some OECD countries, there are now programmatic 'citizens' charters' (as, for example, in Great Britain), and legal guarantees of the position in the market of customers in the shape of democratic participatory rights (for example, by citizens' advisory councils in council structures,[34] or by contracts which regulate democratic participation within the framework of contract management).[35]

In the direct democracy of Switzerland, there are so far no corresponding examples of an empowerment of the citizen by legally or contractually guaranteed opportunities for participation. Nonetheless, initiatives like citizens' bureaus (for example, in Winterthur) are an innovation of NPM since they can organise service at the counter for the citizen in a focussed, speedy and competent manner which is more efficient and more adjusted to requirements and in this way improve the image of the authorities.[36]

For all the political objections of critics to 'consumerism' re-launched by NPM, initiatives such as these nonetheless show that the buzz-word 'customer orientation' brings about improvements in administrative organisations which, without the energy for reform released by NPM, would scarcely have attained the public perception necessary for their realisation.

---

33   F. Naschold/ J. Bogumil, *Modernisierung des Staates. New Public Mangement und Verwaltungsreform* (Opladen: 1998), p. 65.

34   ibid.

35   R. Maes, 'Public Management between Legality and Efficiency. The Case of Belgian Public Administration', Kickert, *Public Management and Administrative Reform*, pp. 199–213.

36   S. Hardmeier/ U. Klöti, *Die Regierungs- und Verwaltungsreform – Reformbereitschaft in der Bevölkerung. UNIVOX-Jahresbericht 'Staat' mit Zusatzfragen im Auftrag der schweizerischen Bundeskanzlei* (Zürich:1996).

Hopes and Difficulties of Democratic Accountability

a. *NPM Management not without reform of Parliament*

NPM is currently seeking, over and above the administrative efforts at customer orientation, political management partners in the parliaments in order to be able to make good its political management claims. Parliaments are to employ the new management instruments, performance agreement and globalised budget, and so adopt a new role for political management.[37] It is only this incipient parliamentary discussion about political management and democratic control of administrative reform which is beginning to involve not simply the customer but also the citizen.[38]

But attempts to overcome conditional management by law and to establish orientation by the demands of final (aim- and results-oriented) management (including the requirements of controlling the achievement of performance),[39] for example, are encountering difficulties. On the one hand, this role has not established itself because parliament in its legislative work concentrates on creating a political consensus for pre-parliamentary decisions as well as checking the state's financial expenditure (in which there is no clear distinction between aims or tasks and expenditure) to the satisfaction of the interests represented in parliament. On the other hand, controlling achievements on the basis of an improved and more detailed system of reporting on the state execution of measures, as newly demanded by government and administration, requires a qualified competence in policy which up until now has not been necessary in this form. Parliament is adopting a cautious attitude to the autonomous claims of the customer

---

37 U. Bolz/ U. Klöti, 'Parlamentarisches Steuern neu erfinden? NPM-Steuerung durch die Bundesversammlung. Ein Diskussionsbeitrag', *Schweiz. Zentralblatt für Staats- und Verwaltungsrecht*, no. 4, 1996. pp. 145–182; D. Brühlmeier. T. Haldemann, P. Mastronardi, K. Schedler, 'New Public Management für das Parlament. Ein Muster Rahmenerlass WOV', *Schweiz. Zentralblatt für Staats- und Verwaltungsrecht*, no. 4, 1998, pp. 145–182.

38 H. J. Bernoulli, 'Parlamentsarbeit unter dem Einfluss neuer Verwaltungsführung, Die Reformen im Kanton Basel-Stadt als Beispiel'. *Neue Zürcher Zeitung*, no. 265, 1998, p. 87.

39 'Verwaltungsreform in der Schweiz – eine Zwischenbilanz', *Herbsttagung der Schweizerischen Gesellschaft für Verwaltungswissenschaft*, 16–17 November 1998.

definition on the part of the administration since established parliamentary interests are being faced with new legitimacy demands based on achievement.

The difficult learning process for a new definition of the role of parliaments requires an expansion of the managerial customer orientation of NPM and its tying in to the interests of the interest groups represented in parliament. The condition for an empowerment of the citizen would probably be that the various administrative and political processes of defining a customer are held autonomously. The customer, as defined in the product portfolios of NPM projects, the addressee of the execution or the member of a professional group important for the state, in short the customer, who comes into contact with the state in a special category, is not identical to the citizen whose rights exceed particular interests. A premature coalition between administrative orientation towards individual customers or groups of customers and the interest groups represented in parliament would thus not expand the possibilities of participatory rights of citizens, but would strengthen the interests of 'functional democracy',[40] which are highly organised in any case and would perpetuate the selective consideration of interests already contained there. The short-circuiting of parliamentary with administrative criteria and indicators of measuring achievement and controlling attainment of goals has been recognised as the risk of independent parliamentary management and control.

Acquiring the necessary skills for management of an administration oriented to effectiveness and putting them into practice demands a considerable learning process from parliamentarians and is associated with much expenditure. Currently, the parliamentarians at all federal levels are working to create the new management principles.[41] To meet the new

---

40   F. Lehner, 'Konkurrenz, Korporatismus, Konkordanz. Politische Vermittlungs-
      strukturen und wirtschaftspolitische Steuerungskapazität in modernen Demokratien',
      in M. Kaase (ed), *Politische Wissenschaft und politische Ordnung* (Opladen: 1986),
      pp. 146–171.
41   Bundesversammlung, *Parlamentarische Behandlung von Leistungsaufträgen und
      Globalbudgets. Richtlinien des Büros des Stände- und Nationalrates vom 28. August
      bzw. 3. September 1998.*

demands, the old demand for a professionalisation of parliaments[42] has once again been heard. Especially for small communities (councils), the new demands could represent an excessive load within the framework of the parliamentary militia system.

The question about the role of the citizen in the parliamentary reform demanded by NPM confronts the managerial direction of the customer concept with a political logic which causes anxiety for many promoters of NPM. Because of this, do the reforms again run the risk of being absorbed by the existing political processes of consensus-building, which are in their view lacking in efficiency and effectiveness without having used the achieved or potential administrative room for freedom?[43]

b. *New Principles of Legitimation by NPM: Transparency and Effectiveness*

The most important yardstick from the point of view of democratic accountability in the transition from bureaucratic to professional management and control[44] is the criterion of the effectiveness of state measures.[45] Even before the high point of NPM, this received a major boost in Switzerland with a national research programme funded by the Federation[46] and this still serves for NPM too as a critical guideline for the conduct of the 'results-oriented public management'. This yardstick is significant because, from the outset, it imparted to the customer orientation of NPM a corrective oriented on the citizen as policy-taker. In line with this yardstick, it is not sufficient simply to make the output (the products) of

42 S. Cattacin/ A. Kühne/ E. Rüegg, 'Neokorporatismus und Ökologisierung von Politik: Die Rolle des Parlaments bei der Reform des institutionellen designs', in *Parlament – 'Oberste Gewalt des Bundes?'. Festschrift der Bundesversammlung zur 700-Jahr-Feier der Eidgenossenschaft* (Bern: 1998), pp. 39–52.

43 K. Schedler, 'The State of Public Management Reforms in Switzerland', in Kickert, *Public Management and Administrative Reform*, pp. 121–40.

44 B. S. Romzek/ M. J. Dubnick, 'Accountability in the Public Sector. Lessons from the Challenger Tragedy', *Public Administration Review*, 47 (1987), 3, pp. 227–38.

45 See also Art. 170 of *Bundesbschluss über eine neue Bundesverfassung*, 18 December 1998.

46 *Nationales Forschungsprogramm 27: Wirksamkeit staatlicher Massnahmen* (Bern: NFP, 1988–1995).

administrations faster and more efficient. Rather they are to be critically assessed on the basis of their social contributions to problem-solving. The increasing importance of professional evaluations of state programmes, measures and projects comes to the fore especially for those areas of state discharge of duty which, in line with NPM, are decentralised or contracted out.[47] The guarantee of democratic accountability requires improved measuring and controlling of performance precisely in areas of great autonomy of action for organisations.

This orientation is supported by the beginnings of an administrative culture which postulates the primacy of the ability to learn by the administration in order to be able to adapt to speedy and complex change.[48] This aim unites critical observers of public administrations and is not disputed either by public employees as the principle behind their activity. In this culture, which is basically reacting to the pressure on the state to save money, it is not sufficient to adjust the opening times of offices to the working hours of customers, or to increase the number of cases dealt with per unit of time or to increase the frequency of public transport. A more urgent concern in recent years has been the political demand to link a better quality of service to the goal of examining the necessity for public commissions, especially to see whether measures reach their goals and whether the expenditure on them can be justified. In the report on subventions by the Federation,[49] as well as in other examinations of commissions in the Federation and in the cantons,[50] this endeavour becomes very clear.

A second theme is linked to this which is praised by many as an original contribution of NPM towards improving the democratic legitimacy of the state. NPM has created new standards of transparency which are to be realised by administrations through a plethora of instruments of information, requested or already in place. At the same time, NPM, in its endeavour to improve information about administrative action through the introduction

---

47   G. E. Caiden/ N. J. Caiden, 'Überwachung, Messung und Evaluierung der Leistung öffentlicher Programme. Ansätze und Massstäbe', *Verwaltung und Management*, 3, 1999, pp.138–46.

48   Eidgenössisches Personalamt, 1998, op.cit.

49   *Bericht des Bundesrates über die Prüfung der Bundessubventionen*, 25 June 1997.

50   For example, *Regierungsrat des Kantons Zürich*, 1998, op. cit.

of a controlling or auditing system, is accompanied by the competitive beginnings of a measuring of effects. Thus, for example, controlling and developing auditing by performance audits[51] is accompanied by the beginnings of an evaluation of state action and of measuring the effectiveness of policy with professional methods (analysis of causalities in effect models).[52] New forms of audit (for example, performance audits), evaluations of state actions or the widespread introduction of checks have, in spite of competing initiatives and quality standards,[53] the common goal of transparent administration.[54] Even NPM projects themselves are now subject to evaluations.[55]

This transparency, which has yet to be created, is, however, faced with unsolved problems. The attempt to create performance indicators and to measure performances by them is not simply subject to the difficulties of political choice and acceptance of indicators of measurement, but also bumps up against thresholds of complexity of the cause and effect situation of state measures which policy analysis has been demonstrating for some considerable time. The instruments, based on the methods of the social sciences, for policy-oriented evaluations therefore quickly cost a lot of money and time. But since administrations are normally under pressure of time, they like turning to simpler means of information like 'checking' (controlling). In practice this has the effect that even results-oriented administrations are content simply with the economic measurement of their

---

51 Eidgenössische Finanzkontrolle, *Leitfaden für Wirtschaftlichkeitsprüfungen*, 1995; OECD, *Performance Auditing and the Modernisation of Government* (Paris: 1996).

52 C-A. Morand 1999; 'Formes et fonctions de l'évaluation législative', *Gesetzgebung heute*, (Bern: Schweizerische Bundeskanzlei 1999), pp. 79–105; W. Bussmann, 'Die Methodik der prospektiven Gesetzesevaluation', *Gesetzgebung heute*, (Bern: Schweizerische Bundeskanzlei 1997), pp. 109–37; W. Bussmann/ U. Klöti/ P. Knöpfel, *Einführung in die Politikevaluation* (Basel/ Frankfurt: 1997).

53 A. Schenker-Wicki, *Moderne Prüfverfahren für komplexe Probleme. Evaluation und Performance Audits im Vergleich* (Wiesbaden: 1999).

54 W.Jann, 'Public Management Reform in Germany. A Revolution without a Theory? in Kickert, *Public Management and Administrative Reform*, pp. 81–101; E. Chelimsky/ W. R. Shadish, *Evaluation for the 21st Century. A Handbook* (London: 1997).

55 T. Haldemann, 'Evaluation von Politik- und Verwaltungsreformen.: Institutionelle und materielle Auswirkungen von NPM- und WOV-Projekten, *Gesetzgebung heute*, 3, 1997, pp. 63–109.

output but do not examine their social contributions to problem-solving (outcomes).[56]

NPM is forcing a development towards the creation of transparency which goes beyond programmatic customer-orientation and is based on high expectations from information on public administrations.[57] It is true that the economic roots of NPM have, in this respect, long since become mixed with professional standards of evaluation and measurement of performance and with political demands for effect-oriented examinations of commissions and performances. The transformation by NPM of the citizen into the customer is to this extent accompanied in the light of policy evaluation by a politically effective reflection of the customer as citizen. It is to the merit of NPM that it has not closed itself off from the demand for evaluations, that it has accepted the offer of reflection from policy analyses and that it has presented itself as a platform for all this. But this requires time which is not planned for in many NPM projects because they are directed towards realisation and hence have tight project schedules. If the products are delayed because of excessive demands, they run the danger of losing their momentum and petering out in the administrations. However much an exacting requirement for effectiveness and a qualitatively high transparency of information instruments become the democratic yardstick for NPM, many projects have, for this very reason, a fear of failing because of shortage of time.

c. NPM and E-Government

The technological development of a 'tele-administration' as a motor for change in administrations improves the chances of NPM being realised. Numerous decentralised initiatives for electronic communication for businesses and government offices are, in conjunction with NPM, aiming for an electronic offer oriented to customer requirements of focussed information and communication as well as an offer of services which also

---

56   M. Zürcher, 'Wider ein betriebswirtschaftlich verkürztes New Public Management. Über Produkte, Indikatoren und die Wirksamkeit', *Gesetzgebung heute*, 2, 1999, pp. 205–35; Caiden/Caiden, op. cit.

57   Jann, op. cit.

makes citizen contact with government offices available online.[58] The basic ideas of an electronic 'one-stop government',[59] for example the creation of virtual citizens' offices, is in line with the aims of NPM.

In the OECD countries, doubters and optimists in the assessment of these new possibilities of an 'e-government' are gathering with a view to advancing administrative reforms by means of the new technology. Were the new potential of technical communication possibilities to be realised, not only must general accessibility of electronic on-line connections be created, but the work processes in the background have to be organised for the citizen in such a way that its results (products) are presented in a manner which corresponds with requirements.[60] In addition, the same technical development encourages possibilities for the transformation of direct democracy in the direction of 'e-democracy' (for example, electronic voting) and of accompanying social trends which promote communication and participation.[61] Although NPM and e-government are at one in aims, it remains to be seen whether the administrations based on division of labour succeed in fulfilling the organisational prerequisites which are demanding, not simply from a technical point of view. Many projects are at the experimental stage.

58   Koordinationsgruppe Informationsgesellschaft , *Bericht an den Bundesrat*, 14 April 1999.
59   H. Kubicek/ M. Hagen, 'Von der Web-Seite zum "One-Stop-Government". Die öffentliche Verwaltung der USA auf dem Information Superhighway', *Verwaltung und Management*, 1998, no. 4, pp.208–13.
60   A.Engel, 'Telekoperation für die öffentliche Verwaltung'. *Verwaltung und Management*, 1999, no. 5, pp. 266–72.
61   H. Geser, 'Auf dem Weg zur "Cyberdemocracy"? Auswirkungen der Computernetze auf die öffentliche-politische Kommunikation', in http://www.unizh.ch/-geserweb/komoef/ftext.html, 1996.

Customers or Citizens? – Three Pictures of the Future

The administrative reforms have so far not brought about a direct strengthening of the role of the citizen. The NPM projects have been too much limited to the function of an internal modernisation for that.[62] It is true that the projects were transferred to the political arena with the question about management by parliaments. But so far, the citizen has been largely untouched by this. An empowerment of the citizen[63] has not yet taken place in this sense.

The discussion about NPM has led meanwhile to a revival of institutional management questions which were foretold without NPM. NPM has provided these questions with a new platform and acts in general as a catalyst for necessary reforms for the manageability of the political system. For many actors,[64] NPM provides opportunities to participate in a modernisation project. About many, possibly decisive, questions these players are not in agreement, however. Thus, in public right-wing and conservative circles have so far succeeded in effectively attributing oppositional political motives to the endeavours of NPM which, from their point of view, seem technocratic. The polarisation between modernisers (those 'open to the world' and those gaining from modernisation) and conservatives (Swiss with a *réduit* mentality or isolationists and those losing by modernisation) is becoming more and more visible across the political spectrum.

Three Pictures of the Future

Switzerland is faced with problems of social and national coherence as well as with those of international integration. In the light of postponed decisions and shortcomings inherent in the system (non-decisions) and their effects, a merely managerial direction to NPM cannot be sufficent to cope

---

62   For example, Naschold, pp. 69–109.
63   Mastronardi/Schedler, pp. 14 and 54.
64   See the introductory section, 'Reception and Perception of NPM in Switzerland'.

with the problems.[65] Nonetheless the effects to date of NPM should not be underestimated. It began to re-organise and to improve in essential elements the administrative infrastructure of the state as an international location factor on all federal levels. Additionally, NPM began to encode the semantics of the political transformation of Switzerland and her conflicts in a new way. It is still an open question as to whether this transformation, within the framework of the political articulation strategies of the players confronting one another on the platform of NPM, will in future carry the code of the high-income, competitive citizen in the sense of an economically restricted NPM, or with the code of the socially-minded citizen in the guarantor state or even in the activating state.

A sketch of three scenarios for administrative reform follows. Whether one or the other development has any chance depends essentially on two factors which are outwith the control of NPM: the pressure for economies from tight budgets within the framework of economic development and the unravelling situation of coalition between the relevant political forces in the discussion about where Switzerland has come from and where she is going (political polarisation between Left and Right). The three pictures of the future are different in the extent to which they realise the NPM reforms which have already begun.

a. *The Discontinuing Reform: NPM as an Element of Economic Liberalism*

Continuing constraints for cuts and the pressure of the market ideologise concepts of state management between neo-liberalism and social state. Political opposition from the Right, which is attracting increasing attention, strengthens neo-liberal concepts of reform when the political system is under growing pressure from problems. The concordance principle for forming governments is at its limits or is disregarded in favour of centre-Right majorities. The content of NPM is reduced to strategies for increasing efficiency. This development in state management is causing the all-party NPM reform coalition to crumble. NPM is becoming a strategy of economic liberalism and is rapidly losing political significance.

---

65   Germann, pp. 274f.

Political polarisation blocks effective reforms by the political system, government and parliament or leads to narrowly technocratic changes in the government system. Thus, the general institutional conditions for NPM are not fulfilled. Increased frustration at the high administrative expenditure, few visible results of management and undesired effects (for example, an increase in the rules governing administrative procedures) have an effect and cause NPM to peter out in the administrations. It is true that an orientation towards effectiveness of state action remains because of the continuing pressure from problems of state management, but this is being replaced by concepts of privatisation and deregulation because of political pressure from conservative and neo-liberal quarters. Deficits in the effectiveness of state management become meaningless because of the dismantling of the state. Continuing pressure for cuts leads to further dismantling of the state.

Within this framework, customer orientation regains its original meaning in the market model of society. Due to new political coalitions of the centre parties with the forces of the Right, the conflicts about distribution are increasing and, supported by direct democratic strategies, are blocking further reforms. The role of the citizen is not being influenced by the model of an exacting customer but is being shaped within the framework of class war by issues from the Left (in the traditional sense) as well as by resurgent social movements.

b. *Partial Reform: NPM as a Building-site for Modernisation*

Despite continuing constraints towards cuts and the pressure of the market on state services and solutions to social problems, the spread of political polarisation between Left and Right and between majorities and minorities to the system of government can be prevented. The concordance and consensus principle of state management remains in place in principle but is suspended in certain cases in favour of majority solutions. Increasingly, traditional management concepts of (neo)liberal and social democratic origin are being joined by solutions within the framework of social self-organisation of a non-profit sector. The guarantor state has opportunities where it can aim for gains in efficiency in conjunction with a reduction of effectiveness deficits. The NPM reform coalition remains with its all-party character. NPM can stabilise itself on this basis in form and programme as a process without fear of disappointment.

NPM becomes noticeable and can create islands of modernisation in the administration. Parliament and government orient themselves pragmatically by the new principles of function and management and partially realise their comprehensively planned parliament and government reforms. The reforms can protect NPM from too much disappointment and frustration on the part of staff. The belief in the basic reformability of the system can therefore remain as the frame to the political challenge and to further learning processes. But the model as a whole loses clarity and momentum because it has to be developed further on the level of individual projects (single-case reform) and in the face of growing opposition. In this framework, formative evaluations to stabilise conflict processes become more important. The institutionalisation of evaluations of state programmes and measures proceeds only cautiously. Continuing pressure to make cuts and political pressure from conservative and neo-liberal circles produces more privatisation. The appropriate political forces seek with NPM to improve the administrative infrastructure especially in order to make Switzerland a more attractive economic place of business.

It is true that customers, as founders of small and middle-sized businesses, international business people and others become or remain from this point of view in practice privileged addressee groups of the state. Nonetheless, it is possible to maintain in essence the basis of the legitimacy of the guarantor state and to find a compromise formula for neo-liberal and social democratic aims. The customer propagated by NPM is within this framework also addressed in his/her role as citizen to strive for socially-minded solutions in favour of minorities within the framework of a responsible society which organises for itself. Organisations in the tertiary sector remain a central management resource of the state which increasingly withdraws from its own management of the fulfillment of state functions. From the basic concepts of customer and citizen, which remain differentiated, the concordance culture will seek to create a mix which is capable of a consensus and is legitimised in law.

c. *The Reform which Succeeds: NPM as a Political Vision*

On the basis of a positive economic development, the state is dispensed from the necessity of making cuts. Political polarisation recedes to make way for consensus solutions to central problems on the basis of the concordance system. The guarantor state is expanded on all levels and acquires greater significance as a procedural arbitrator in arenas for non-state players. The all-party NPM reform coalition sees itself confirmed in its endeavours to meet the basic need for reform of the political and administrative system and gains political influence.

Because of this influence essential reforms of parliament and government are successful. Parliament assumes a new management role oriented towards aims whilst government unburdens itself of administrative tasks in favour of functions of strategic leadership. On these institutional bases, NPM can be successfully realised. Orientation towards effectiveness establishes itself as the norm. Evaluations of state programmes and measures become increasingly institutionalised and regarded as a matter of course.

The gains for the country as a place of business and for the economy as a result of the modernisation of the state are combined with the model of the guarantor state. Alongside the new customer orientation, the principle of solidarity can develop in new forms of social self-management and prevent minorities from being marginalised. The concept of the customer is expanded and additionally strengthens the position of the citizen by providing new legal and contractual possibilities for participation beyond direct democratic 'customer questionnaires'. It is true that this process is accompanied by further privatisation of state services. But the basic achievements of the social and welfare state can be retained and can be provided in new types of state management in a more efficient manner and in a manner better suited to requirements and to those at whom they are directed. A stop can be put to the erosion of national and social cohesion.

Translated by Malcolm Pender

MALCOLM PENDER

Unrealised Visions of the Future:
Max Frisch and *achtung: Die Schweiz*

One of the best-known photographs of Max Frisch shows him on a building site, a pencil in his right hand and a piece of paper in his left, demonstrating a point to Bertolt Brecht who is looking on attentively.[1] The photograph must date from before October 1948, when Brecht left Zürich after a stay of some months on his way from United States exile to East Germany, and the building site is that of the public open-air swimming pool Letzigraben in Zürich during the period of its construction from August 1947 to June 1949. Frisch had won the competition for the design of the pool shortly after setting up in practice as an architect in 1943, but construction was delayed due to circumstances of war. Letzigraben was the one major building of the four realised by Frisch during his fourteen years as an architect,[2] and it was the subject of eleven entries in Frisch's first major successful book, *Tagebuch 1946–1949*, published by Suhrkamp in Germany in 1950. The photograph, embodying the activities of discussion, explanation and questioning in relation to practical realisation, is a pictorial representation of central aspects of Frisch's outlook as an architect and writer. In the late 1940s and early 1950s particularly, Frisch contributed to many contemporary debates, arguably achieving most public resonance with his involvement in the visionary pamphlet *achtung: Die Schweiz*, published in 1955. It is worthwhile setting the pamphlet in the context of Frisch's views and activities as an architect and writer at the time for

1   The photograph is, for example, on the cover of the book edited by Julian Schütt, *Max Frisch. Jetzt ist Sehenszeit. Briefe, Notate, Dokumente 1943–1963* (Frankfurt am Main: 1998).
2   Cf Urs Bircher, *Vom langsamen Wachsen eines Zorns. Max Frisch 1911–1955* (Zürich: 1997), p. 211; for a complete depiction of Frisch's buildings, competition entries and unrealised projects, see the 'Werkkatalog' in Petra Hagen, *Städtebau im Kreuzverhör. Max Frisch zum Städtebau der fünfziger Jahre* (Baden (CH): 1986), pp. 100–118.

achtung: Die Schweiz provides an interesting example of the relationship between reality and Utopia.

At the close of his provisional 'Autobiographie', drawn up in the summer of 1948 as an assertion of identity in Paris, a city in which it is impossible to do anything 'was nicht Millionen schon getan haben' (II 583),[3] Frisch comments that 'die Ausübung eines doppelten Berufes' has, in spite of difficulties, 'segensreiche Wirkungen'. One of the positive aspects is that, as an architect, he deals daily with people who have nothing to do with literature. Clearly, he is referring to his current involvement with the Letzigraben project. Yet if he is here emphasising differences between the two spheres of activity, other statements provide parallels between them. Thus, in a passage in *Tagebuch 1946–1949* specifically relating to Letzigraben, Frisch proclaims his liking for the half-complete:

> Es ist mir am ganzen Bauen eigentlich das liebste: Rohbau, bevor die Dächer gedeckt sind. Backstein und Holz, lauter Räume voll Himmel, den man durch alle Stockwerke sieht. (II 593)

Earlier, Frisch had voiced his approval for the fact that 'die Skizze' had come back as a literary form since this was the expression of a receptive, open attitude:

> Die Skizze als Ausdruck eines Weltbildes, das sich nicht mehr schließt oder noch nicht schließt; als Scheu vor einer förmlichen Ganzheit, die der geistigen vorauseilt' (II 448).

In 1945, in the story *Bin oder Die Reise nach Peking*, Frisch had expressed his frustration at the manner in which the physical reality of a project flaunted its difference to what had been planned, writing of the 'Hohn der Verwirklichung, dieser feindselige und bösartige Eigensinn alles Fertigen' (I 635). In 1948, as he contemplates the nearly complete building of Letzigraben, he is depressed by its immutability: 'Alles wird eisern und steinern, endgültig, es gibt nichts mehr zu wollen' (II 618). Yet the opposite end of the process, the point at which there is nothing, has its own particular torment. The stimulation for Frisch of Brecht's two-hour visit to the Letzigraben site is precisely that Brecht knows of this latter difficulty and

---

3   References are to *Max Frisch. Gesammelte Werke in zeitlicher Folge*, ed. by Hans Mayer, 7 vols (Frankfurt am Main: 1976–86).

Frisch makes the general point: 'der Schaffende, gleichviel wo er selber wirkt, weiß um das leere Papier' (II 638). And if the empty page creates a link between the architect and the writer, as did the potential of what is incomplete, the writer also has a link to another practitioner with material reality, the sculptor, for 'die Sprache ist wie ein Meißel': as the chisel of the sculptor works its way into the stone, in a similar fashion 'arbeitet die Sprache, indem sie die Leere, das Sagbare, vortreibt gegen das Geheimnis' (II 379); and the parallel with the sculptor is extended further:

> Immer besteht die Gefahr, daß man das Geheimnis zerschlägt, und ebenso die andere Gefahr, daß man vorzeitig aufhört, daß man es einen Klumpen sein läßt, daß man das Geheimnis nicht stellt (II 379)

All three professions – architect, writer, sculptor – are linked by the paradoxes inherent in creativity, by the problems of realising a vision.

It is appropriate at this point to review in outline the double strand of activity conducted by Frisch as architect and writer at the end of the 1940s and in the first half of the 1950s, the period which closed with the publication of *achtung: Die Schweiz,* and which exemplifies, possibly more than any other in his long life, his attempts to impart substance in reality to ideas. In January 1949, the play *Als der Krieg zu Ende war* was premiered and in June Letzigraben was opened. At the beginning of 1950, Frisch submitted a design for a lakeside swimming-pool at Horgen on the Zürichsee,[4] in September *Tagebuch 1946–1949* was published and work began in Schaan on a country-house to Frisch's design. In February 1950, the first version of the play *Graf Öderland* had its premiere, and in April Frisch went to the United States on a Rockefeller scholarship and worked there on *Stiller* and the play *Don Juan oder Die Liebe zur Geometrie.* He returned to Zürich in May 1952, and worked on the 'Hörspiel' *Herr Biedermann und die Brandstifter* (broadcast March 1953). In the spring of 1953 he wrote a second 'Hörspiel' *Rip van Winkle* (broadcast in June that year), *Don Juan* was premiered in May, in June he delivered the speech *Cum grano salis* to the Zürich branch of the Swiss Architects Association, in the summer worked on the closing stages of *Stiller,* was approached by Markus Kutter and Lucius Burckhardt for whose pamphlet, *Wir selber bauen unsere Stadt,* he wrote a foreword (published in September), and in

---

4   See Hagen, p. 107, for the reasons why the project did not come to fruition.

November Frisch submitted a design for an extension to the physics building of the University of Zürich. At the beginning of 1954, he participated in a competition for the design of the Kantonsschule Freudenberg in Zürich, in the course of the year he radically re-cast a second draft pamphlet brought to him by Kutter and Burckhardt, in October *Stiller* was published, work was done on a project for a 'Künstlersiedlung' in Zürich and a 'Hörspiel', *Der Laie und die Architektur*, was drafted (prize awarded March 1955, broadcast May 1955). In January 1955, the second pamphlet involving Burckhardt and Kutter was published with the title *achtung: Die Schweiz*, Frisch gave up his practice and in the summer of 1955 addressed an international conference of architects in Denver, Colorado. An assessment of the reaction to *achtung: Die Schweiz* was published as *Die neue Stadt. Beiträge zur Diskussion* in 1956.

It is not surprising that this intensive creative activity – arguably Frisch's most productive period – gave rise to cross-fertilisation, causing similar ideas to appear in different contexts in different kinds of publication. It is important to realise, when Frisch's contribution to *achtung: Die Schweiz* is being set in context, that this particular involvement was entirely of a piece with Frisch's general outlook and concerns of the time. Thus his stay in the United States from 1951 to 1952, in a fashion similar to the way in which his travels in war-ravaged Europe immediately after the German capitulation in May 1945 had altered his political outlook, strongly influenced the perspective from which he viewed Swiss architecture and the Swiss political ethos. Two documents relating to architecture and city planning, *Cum grano salis,* which preceded work on *achtung: Die Schweiz*, and *Der Laie und die Architektur*, work on which must have been proceeding when *achtung: Die Schweiz* was going to publication, establish the point.

Cum grano salis, delivered as a lecture in June 1953 and published in October 1953, exactly a year before the publication of the novel *Stiller*, shows similarities of outlook and wording with the latter.[5] A striking feature of *Cum grano salis* is the manner in which Frisch, like Anatol Stiller, presents his views from the perspective of a person who has been out of

5   See Walter Schmitz, 'Zur Entstehung von Max Frischs Roman "Stiller"', in *Materialien zu Max Frisch 'Stiller'*, edited by Walter Schmitz (Frankfurt am Main: 1978), pp. 29–34 (p. 34, footnote 14) for exact details of the textual parallels.

Switzerland – within the relatively short text the phase 'der Heimkehrende' occurs sixteen times. Switzerland appears to the returnee to be in the grip of a nostalgia for the past, 'Heimweh nach dem Vorgestern' (III 236), her people united only by the hope that the Russians will not come. Frisch seeks to highlight the dangerous negativity of this aspiration by asking rhetorically what aim the Swiss have beyond this: 'Was ist, wenn die Russen uns erspart blieben, unser eigentliches Ziel? Was wollen wir aus unserem Land gestalten?' (III 236), a technique of posing questions to the reader which adumbrates that of *achtung: Die Schweiz*.[6] Frisch then goes back to a key date in the Swiss past, 1848, where he finds what is lacking in the present, vision and confidence: 'Damals hatten sie einen Entwurf... und freuten sich auf das Übermorgen' (III 236). Today, on the other hand, the concept of tradition has been traduced to the extent that 'ein architektonisches Epigonentum' (III 237) holds sway; it is after all absurd to imagine that the political liberty achieved by the generations of 1848 is a static matter: 'Der schweizerische Wahn, man sei frei wie die Väter, indem man nicht über die Väter hinauszugehen wagt' (III 240); equally certainly, these earlier generations did not intend the 'Freiheit der Mächtigen' (III 240) which obtains today in the exploitation of land and building regulations, political change lies 'allein in unserer Hand' (III 239). Frisch's challenge, 'Haben wir keine Ideen? (III 241), is directed at his audience both in their capacity as architects and as contemporaries – he is seeking 'die Möglichkeit einer lebendigen Schweiz' (III 242).

   Der Laie und die Architektur, broadcast on 14 May 1955 in the 'Hessischer Rundfunk' but conceived concurrently with the work on *achtung: Die Schweiz*, also bears the hallmarks of the time spent by Frisch out of Switzerland in that three foreign cities – Frankfurt am Main, Mexico City and Marseilles – figure in what is termed *Ein Funkgespräch*. 'Der Laie', in the company of his wife and 'der Architekt', discuss architecture and visit, by means of a magic carpet, sites in the three cities which exemplify aspects of the discussion. The view that architecture is a community responsibility is advanced even more forcefully than in *Cum grano salis*. In an increasingly particularised world, the layman insists that the expert – in this case the architect – has no right to dictate solutions, instead he has the duty to place his skills at the service of the community:

6   See Hagen, p. 82, for a discussion of Frisch's use of questions.

'Die Aufgaben stellt nicht der Fachmann, sondern immer der Laie; der Fachmann löst sie. Oder sagen wir statt Laie: die Gemeinschaft aller Laien, die Gesellschaft, die Polis' (III 264). The layman is quite clear that urban development implies involvement which is all-embracing: 'Städtebau ist ein politisches Anliegen. Ein Anliegen der Polis' (III 264). Frankfurt am Main, in the view of the layman, bears a depressing similarity with Switzerland in that the rebuilding of the bombed area around the cathedral has been carried out as if people believe 'daß sie damit die Goethe-Zeit zurückbringen können' (III 373); the architect is in broad agreement, dismissing the restoration as 'Kosmetik' (III 272) and suggesting that 'ein großer Park' (III 273) round about the cathedral would both have set off its particular architectural qualities and recognised openly that the city had been visited by war.[7] In Mexico City, on the other hand, buildings have been constructed in a contemporary idiom: the architect is 'beglückt zu sehen, wieviel einer modernen Architektur möglich ist, sobald sie einmal den Mut zu sich selbst hat', and he enthuses: 'Wieviel Gestalt, wieviel Gesicht, wieviel lebendige Aussage!' (III 273). Le Corbusier's recently constructed 'Unité d'Habitation' in Marseilles, containing 337 flats arranged in '23 verschiedene Wohnungstypen' (III 284) – is a planned building permitting variety, 'eine Wohneinheit, aber nicht als Dörflein romantisiert' (III 285). For the layman, the building symbolises positive planning which harnesses the vitality of creative forces in the realisation of a vision, 'die produktive Planung, die nicht verbietet, sondern verlockt, Anreize in die Welt setzt und zu Taten führt' (III 288). The same spirit of creative enterprise informs *achtung: Die Schweiz*.

Frisch had already collaborated with Lucius Burckhardt and Markus Kutter in 1953, but *Wir selber bauen unsere Stadt*, a pamphlet on town planning with particular reference to Basel, had attracted little attention.[8] In the summer of 1954, Burckhardt and Kutter again approached Frisch with a manuscript which was focussed specifically on the 'Landes-ausstellung' projected for 1964. Frisch was requested to re-formulate the wording of the document which had been discussed amongst architects.

---

7   In the autumn of 1955, Frisch was to characterise the 'Wiederaufbau-Katastrophe' in Germany as 'für den Städtebau schlimmer als die Bomben-Katastrophe', in 'Wer liefert ihnen denn die Pläne?', III 346–54 (347).

8   Bircher, p. 230.

Thus, *achtung: Die Schweiz,* published in January 1955, was a collaborative project for which Burckhardt furnished the title.[9] Mindful of the fate of *Wir selber bauen unsere Stadt,* the collaborators took the decision to make an impact, depicting on the red cover a white cross, 'eine Landesikone',[10] and casting the material in a provocative style as Frisch stated years later:'[wir] haben [...] bewusst auf die Pauke gehauen und polemisch formuliert'.[11] Indeed, it is possible to claim that the writing bears the hallmarks of Frisch's re-working of the original text: 'Unstreitig ist der ironisch verknappte, politisch angriffige Stil Frischs Werk'.[12] And whilst the main proposal of the pamphlet for the construction of a 'Musterstadt' was not new in Switzerland since it had previously been propagated there as something already realised in the British 'New Towns',[13] much of the thinking and many of the formulations in *achtung: Die Schweiz* accord with the work already discussed which Frisch was publishing at the start of the 1950s.

The wide framework of reference to *achtung: Die Schweiz* is implicit in the sub-title, *Ein Gespräch über unsere Lage und ein Vorschlag zur Tat,* and the notion of discussion and debate is reinforced by an indication of the number of people who have been involved in preliminary consultation.[14] The matter addressed is from the outset placed firmly in the context of contemporary world politics in the mid-1950s, when the Cold War, during which Switzerland was more than anxious to display her anti-Communist credentials, was at its height. In the view of *achtung; Die Schweiz,* the confrontation between the ideological blocs acquires the widest existential connotations, since it addresses 'die wesentlichen Fragen unserer menschlichen Existenz' (III 293); the struggle is not one of

---

9   See *Gesammelte Werke* (III 864) and Markus Kutter, 'Achtung: die Schweiz', *Die Weltwoche,* 31 December 1998.
10   Bircher, p. 230.
11   Arthur Zimmermann, 'Polemik – Ein Gespräch mit Max Frisch', in *Max Frisch, Dossier Reihe Literatur 2* (Zürich/Bern: 1981), pp. 39–45 (p. 39).
12   Bircher, p. 231.
13   Hagen, p. 38.
14   'Diese Broschüre ist das Ergebnis einer Diskussion zwischen Lucius Burckhardt, Max Frisch und Markus Kutter unter Zuzug der Architekten Rolf Gutmann und Theo Manz, sowe zweier Vertreter der Wirtschaft, eines Staatsbeamten und eines Kantonalen Parlamentariers' (III 291).

straightforward 'Machtpolitik': it is a 'Kampf der Ideen' which is simultaneously 'ein Kampf um die Lebensform in unserer Zeit' (III 293). The magnitude of the matter creates an unusual situation for the Swiss[15] in that there is no possibility of neutrality: 'In der Auseinandersetzung um die Lebensform gibt es keinen Neutralismus' (III 294). The question 'Wo in dieser großen Auseinandersetzung...steht die Schweiz, unsere Heimat?' (III 295) can only be properly discussed if the notion is put aside that 'Selbstkritik'and 'Verrat' (III 296) are synonymous terms. Switzerland, faced with this challenge, is portrayed by the brochure as being in a state of inertia, incapable of formulating responses appropriate to the world which the Second World War has left behind. This has to do, not so much with lack of ideas, but with their realisation, 'Schwierigkeiten beim Schritt von der Idee zur Ausführung' which is ironic since Switzerland is itself 'nichts anderes als eine Idee, die einmal realisiert worden ist'(III 297). And, in a clear reference to a widespread Swiss self-perception, the pamphlet insists, in a sentence which was to become well-known, on the primacy of the idea: 'Man ist nicht realistisch, indem man keine Idee hat' (III 297). The last time Switzerland realised such an idea was in the creation of the 'Landesausstellung' of 1939, an event which was not simply a rejection of Fascism but which also brought together divergent political strands of the Swiss nation in a common vision, as had 1848. At both historical points, a sense of purposeful unity had been present – 'der Wille zum Handeln, die Fähigkeit zum Handeln' (III 299). Yet whilst the brochure is unstinting in its praise of the 'Landesausstellung' as an example – 'was 1939 Vorbild war, wirklich wegweisende Leistung, sollte Vorbild bleiben – diskussionslos' (III 300)[16] – it also insists that that achievement 'ist historisch geworden' (III 297), that it was 'die Manifestation unserer Väter' (III 301). And the first two sections of the ten which constitute the pamphlet close with the question: 'Welche soll die unsere sein?' (III 301). Thus the question confronted by Frisch in his architectural and literary work – the realisation of ideas – is seen as lying at the core of Swiss history.

15   The notion of discussion is sustained throughout by the use of the first person plural when the Swiss are mentioned.

16   Interestingly, Markus Kutter, in his *Weltwoche* article over forty years later, when perceptions of 1939 have altered, takes the same positive view of the 'Landes-ausstellung': 'Ein Wille zur kompromisslosen Modernität herrschte vor', 'Achtung: die Schweiz'.

The next three sections excoriate, in a manner familiar from *Cum grano salis* and *Der Laie und die Architektur*, the feeble-minded inertia which Frisch perceives to be paralysing Switzerland. Being spared damage and being prosperous ('die Konjunktur, die unser Land dominiert und deformiert' (III 295)) deflect Swiss attention from more radical concerns: 'Die Schweiz als Ganzes, so scheint es, ist keine Aufgabe mehr' (III 304).[17] And in a sentence reflecting the sentiment behind the title suggested by Frisch for the pamphlet, *Ist die Schweiz eine Mumie?*,[18] Frisch portrays how the idea of Switzerland has been reduced to the level of an absurd historical charade without relation to the present:

> Wir verlieren nur die Lebensform der Vorfahren, zwangsläufig, wir mumifizieren sie in Festen; das Schweizertum wird zum Kostüm, das als Kostüm gepflegt wird. (III 306)

And the conclusion about the disjunction between static attitudes and the process of reality is blunt: 'Für die Neuzeit haben wir keine Lebensform' (III 306). In an echo of an accusation familiar from both *Cum grano salis* and *Stiller*, Switzerland is guilty of living in a present imbued with a fear for the future since the future threatens the stability of perceptions of the past. In the face of this philosophical vacuum, the pamphlet exhorts its readers to re-define the notion of Switzerland in contemporary terms:

> Wir wollen kein schweizerisches Minderwertigkeitsgefühl, keinen schweizerischen Größenwahn; sondern wir wollen eine Schweiz, die sich selbst ins Gesicht zu schauen wagt, eine Schweiz, die sich nicht vor der Wandlung scheut, eine Schweiz, die ihre Idee an den heutigen Problemen und mit den heutigen Mitteln zu verwirklichen sucht. (III 308)

The ensuing exhortation to his fellow Swiss is one which Frisch sustained from the late 1940s virtually to the end of his life: 'Wir wollen die Schweiz als eine Aufgabe' (III 308). The present time is perceived by the brochure as being in breach of the spirit of the past which respected and realised

---

17 Ten years later Frisch was to return to the same topic in respect of contemporary Swiss literature in his famous essay 'Unbewältigte schweizerische Vergangenheit' (1965) (V 370–3).

18 See III 864; Kutter confirms that the final title was proposed by Burckhardt, 'Achtung: die Schweiz'.

ideas. For this reason, the abrupt challenge of its title represents a call for a resumption of a worthy tradition.

The proposition to establish a new town is made within this historical and ethical framework. Additionally, the experimental nature of the venture is stressed: the town

> soll uns zeigen, ob wir noch eine lebendige Idee haben, eine Idee, die eine Wirklichkeit zu zeugen vermag, eine schöpferische Vorstellung von unserer Lebensform in dieser Zeit. (III 309)

But first of all it will be necessary to discard or re-think at least three unexamined assumptions which relate to building development. Firstly, the notion that towns develop 'organically' is incorrect because all developments have in fact been planned by one of two agencies: 'die Spekulation oder der Staat' (III 314). Secondly, there has been a blurring of the distinction between town and village: 'Wir bauen im dörflichen Maßstab, bis das Dorf eben eine Stadt ist, aber eine Stadt mit dörflicher Bauweise' (III 312). The consequence of this is that the advantages of a planned modern city are lost. Thirdly, planning is widely held to be quite incompatible with cherished Swiss notions of freedom. But the signatories to the pamphlet hold that the existing *laissez-faire* situation is equally incompatible with any idea of real freedom: 'Wir sind der Meinung, daß die Freiheit nicht in einem freien Laufenlassen der Dinge besteht' (III 315). Planning, erroneously perceived as an attribute of totalitarian regimes, is in fact the arbiter of real freedom and the Swiss should accept the necessity of planning before it is too late: 'Nicht durch die Russen gezwungen, sondern durch die Geschichte der Freiheit!' (III 314); again, this is seen as the resumption of a historical continuity. The manner in which Swiss assumptions are subjected to rigorous and challenging scrutiny adumbrates a similar examination of Swiss myths in Frisch's *Wilhelm Tell für die Schule* of 1970 and attests to Frisch's influence on the formulation and style of *achtung: Die Schweiz.*

There now follow quite precise specifications in relation to the experimental town. It is to be planned for approximately 15,000 inhabitants and four possible sites are suggested: in the triangle between the Lakes of Biel, Murten and Neuchâtel, in the delta of the Rhône, in the Canton of Fribourg or in the Canton of Aargau. There would be a central provision of heating for both industrial and domestic purposes and every profession which had to do with the construction of the new town would be asked:

'Was würden Sie unternehmen, wenn Sie einmal verwirklichen könnten, was Sie wollen?' (III 325). Industrial and commercial undertakings would be admitted to the new town to the extent that they were capable of demonstrating that they were socially responsible employers. A draft framework for the legal entity which would regulate the assembly of the myriad elements combining to constitute the new town is set forth, as are the broad outlines of the manner in which the venture would be financed. And the new town is in its entirety to constitute the next 'Landesausstellung' scheduled for 1964.[19] One major reason for this suggestion is that the town would then directly reflect the reality of modern Switzerland: 'Wir zeigen die Schweiz nicht als Pavillon, sondern als Ernstfall – im Maßstab 1 : 1' (III 327). A second reason would be the influence of the quality of the new town as a 'Landesausstellung'. At this point the reader recalls that the novel *Stiller* demonstrated, in its presentation of the theme of *Reproduktion*, the nefarious influence on the individual of patterns of behaviour emanating from fashion and the media, for it is here now suggested that the new town could have a positive influence on his comportment. Since most people simply adopt the 'Lebensart' which is currrently in vogue, 'das Vorbild, das Leitbild' (III 321) provided by the town as an exhibition would have a beneficial effect on the lifestyle of those adopting it. The whole undertaking would represent 'ein geistiges Wagnis' (III 332).

achtung: Die Schweiz, with 10,000 copies sold – an extraordinarily high figure at the time for Switzerland – was one of the most discussed publications of the 1950s in the country.[20] Yet, despite the fact that the authors received over 1,000 letters, 95 per cent of which approved the proposal, the resonance, especially in the press which produced over 200 articles on the subject, was far from being uniformly benevolent. Over forty years later, Markus Kutter recalls the tenor of the negative reactions:

> Wahnsinn, fundamentales Missverständnis in Sachen organisches Wachstum, Föderalismus, Gemeindefreiheit. Begütigende, belehrende, erzürnte, bösartige, spöttische Stimmen.[21]

---

19   This part of the proposal was later dropped, cf. *Die neue Stadt* (1956), the third pamphlet issued by the trio Burckhardt, Frisch and Kutter in which the public reaction to *achtung: Die Schweiz* is discussed.

20   See Hagen, pp. 76–7, and Bircher, pp. 231–35.

21   Kutter, 'Achtung: die Schweiz'.

It was not that the proposal itself was radically new and thus difficult to accept, for the suggestion for a new town was to a large extent following in the wake of the New Towns already in train in Great Britain. Rather it was Frisch's 'sprachliche Beherrschung der Materie und der klugen sprachlich-didaktischen Form seiner Polemiken'[22] which caught public attention and, in some quarters, gave rise to outrage. Frisch had learned from the reaction to the passages in *Stiller* critical of Switzerland about the extreme sensitivity of a highly conservative public to attempts to call any aspect of the country in question. The third pamphlet, *Die Neue Stadt*, sought to continue a dialogue with the public by responding to the reaction to *achtung: Die Schweiz*, and by justifying some of the original argument in the light of comment but, as Frisch later claimed: 'Es fehlte die konstruktive Widerrede'.[23] It became clear that there was no likelihood of the project being realised, even when it was uncoupled from the 'Landesausstellung' of 1964. It was perhaps inevitable that the proposal would founder on 'die Konzeptionslosigkeit der schweizerischen Gesellschaft der 50er Jahre'[24] whose horizons were bounded by anti-Communism and material prosperity.

In 1964, the year of the 'Landesausstellung' in Lausanne, Frisch laments the lost opportunity to confront and shape the reality of contemporary Switzerland: what was required was 'eine aktuelle Tat, nicht eine Ausstellung, wo das Volk sich in einer geschminkten Vergangenheit bespiegeln kann'.[25] But in a wider sense, Switzerland had lost an opportunity to act as as a mediating forum between the ideological attitudes of the two world power blocs, to create what Frisch calls 'ein geistiges Genf'.[26] And over thirty years after that, Markus Kutter confirms the narrow

---

22 Hagen, p. 81.
23 Zimmermann, 'Polemik – Ein Gespräch mit Max Frisch', p. 39; in the same interview, Frisch contrasts the situation almost a decade later, when, after the publication of his essay on foreign workers, Frisch was invited to address a group of cantonal heads of the *Fremdenpolizei*.
24 Walter Obschlager, 'Zeitgenossenschaft. Ein Nachwort', in *Max Frisch – Schweiz als Heimat? Versuche über 50 Jahre* (Frankfurt am Main: 1990), pp. 555–76 (p. 564).
25 Paul Ignaz Vogel, 'Und die Schweiz? Ein Interview mit Max Frisch' [*neutralität* 2 (1964), Heft 5, pp. 2–6], in *Max Frisch – Schweiz als Heimat? Versuche über 50 Jahre*, pp. 205–14 (p. 206).
26 ibid, p. 208.

perspective of the Lausanne exhibition: it was limited to being a 'Landes-ausstellung der Hochkonjunktur',[27] exactly the economic situation which, in the words of *achtung: Die Schweiz*, 'unser Land dominiert und deformiert' (III 295). Acidly, Kutter recalls how the organisers of the 1964 exhibition simply went their own way irrespective of all debate:

> Ungerührt stellten sie ein Konzept auf die Beine, das dann unter dem Motto 'croire et créer pour la Suisse de demain' realisiert wurde. An was zu glauben wäre, blieb unbestimmt; was zu schaffen sei, verstand sich als beschleunigte Fortsetzung dessen, was noch herumstand.[28]

Ironically, *achtung: Die Schweiz* had foreseen the possibility of just such an outcome when the text insisted that the Swiss Federation treat the proposed new town as a living entity and not as a public relations exercise:

> Es kommt also nicht in Frage, daß der Bund diese neue Stadt als schweizerische Reklame subventioniert; wir wollen keine Potemkin-schen Dörfer. (Wenn wir ein Potemkinsches Dorf wollen, dann mache man eben eine Landesausstellung mit Attrapen, ein Propaganda-Schweizchen, die zweite Auflage eines provisorischen Höhenwegs mit kunstgewerblich-gerissener Selbstbeweihräucherung). (III 332–3)

By a further irony, hindsight has shown that the absence of overall planning has not improved the quality of life for the inhabitants of urban develop-ments and also that the problems raised in *achtung: Die Schweiz* have remained unsolved.[29]

In an article, 'Die Schweiz ist ein Land ohne Utopie', which appeared five years after the publication of *achtung: Die Schweiz*, Frisch asks his Swiss readers if they have not noticed 'daß das Wort 'Utopie' bei uns ausschließlich im negativen Sinn verwendet wird?', and, returning to a theme of *achtung: Die Schweiz*, he concludes that this is ironic for 'gerade die Schweiz ist aus nichts anderem als einem utopischen Gedanken entstanden' (IV 258). An interview given in the Ticino in the 1980s contains Frisch's definition of Utopia: 'Die Utopie besteht darin, zu glauben, daß

27 Kutter, 'Achtung; die Schweiz'.
28 ibid.
29 Cf. Hagen, p. 95 and Bircher, p. 235.

die Dinge auch anders gehen könnten'.[30] It is interesting to relate these views, expressed in the years following the failure of *achtung: Die Schweiz* to stimulate action, with Frisch's last public stock-taking, his address to the 'Solothurner Literaturtage' in 1986. Frisch, well into his seventies, asked the question: 'Wie steht ein Schriftsteller, wenn er lange lebt, zu seinen veröffentlichten Hoffnungen?'[31] In this respect, he admits to being 'enttäuscht über den Lauf der Welt', but more serious is his perception that responses to the world are now conditioned by belief and are not the product of clear-sighted cognition: 'Man möchte nicht wissen, sondern glauben'.[32] For this reason, the inheritance of the Enlightenment must be re-defined: 'Aufklärung heute ist Revolte gegen den Aberglauben in die Technologie, die den Menschen antiquiert', He concludes that the sole determining factor in the world is economic gain: 'Am Ende der Aufklärung also steht nicht, wie Kant und die Aufklärer alle hofften, der mündige Mensch, sondern das Goldene Kalb'.[33] More specifically in relation to Switzerland, he sees the country's non-participation in the United Nations as also being determined by economic thinking 'um ja nie verpflichtet zu sein (als Nation) zu einem Akt internationaler Solidarität, die vielleicht dem Finanzplatz Schweiz nicht genehm wäre'.[34] The vision expressed in *achtung: Die Schweiz* seems, against this background, to be Utopian in the Swiss sense of being unrealisable. Thirty years on, it appears that the rupture with the Swiss tradition highlighted in 1955 has become permanent.

Finally, *achtung: Die Schweiz* can be compared with *Stiller*, the novel whose publication preceded that of the pamphlet by a few months. In a famous statement made in Hamburg in 1948, Frisch takes issue with what he feels is a mark of the German tradition, a disjunction between the creative imagination and the state of society, which has been tragically thrown into very sharp focus by the Nazi era; he is moved to affirm a different Swiss tradition which lays strong emphasis on social responsibility, albeit at the expense of the concerns of the creative imagination (II 631). Ironically,

30   Interview with Lina Bertola, 'L'arte è il luogotenente dell'utopia', *Corriere del Ticino*, 30 September 1983, quoted in Hagen, p. 9 (German translation by Hagen).
31   Max Frisch, 'Am Ende der Aufklärung steht das Goldene Kalb', in *Max Frisch – Schweiz als Heimat? Versuche über 50 Jahre*, pp. 461–69 (p. 461).
32   ibid, p. 461.
33   ibid, p. 463.
34   ibid, p. 468.

however, it seems that the works of the creative imagination, far more than the political stances taken on contemporary events and conditions, contain disruptive energy, disruptive not in any trivial manner, but in the sense that the very basis of existing existential assumptions are shaken. For if the 1950s were arguably the most productive decade of Max Frisch's creative life in the sense that the level and quality of both his literary work and his engagement in public issues were never again jointly to attain quite the same intensity and impact, it is, almost half a century later, the literary work of the period which is still being read, whereas the non-literary statements, such as *achtung: Die Schweiz*, have simply become historical documents. Peter von Matt has demonstrated this point precisely in relation to *Stiller*. Opening the Frisch exhibition in Zürich in September 1998 at the point where the disturbance caused by the international deconstruction of the Swiss image of themselves during World War Two was beginning to subside, von Matt refers to the manner in which *Stiller* characterised the contemporary state of Switzerland on its publication, and he continues:

> Und Jahrzehnte später kann dieser Roman für das gleiche Land wieder eine Warnung werden vor dem Versuch, sich nach einer schweren Krise so rasch wie möglich eine neue Nische zu suchen, gut temperiert, mit reduziertem Denkbedarf und erhöhten Marktchancen.[35]

It has been claimed that Gottfried Keller's works reflect continuously throughout his writing career an awareness of 'der inneren Fragwürdigkeit des Saeculums'[36] which was to come only much later in life to Keller the politician. Perhaps the same might be said of Frisch. But perhaps Frisch was aware also of the durability of the creative work of art as opposed to the ephemerality of the political pamphlet. Perhaps for that reason, many of the formulations of Frisch's social and political writings of the 1950s, not least of *achtung: Die Schweiz*, are included in *Stiller*. For, as Frisch himself said: 'Die Kunst ist der Statthalter der Utopie'.[37]

---

35 Peter von Matt, 'Wer zeigt, was es, geschlagen hat? Über die Unerbittlichkeit der Kunst und wie man sie zu entschärfen sucht', reprinted in *Der Stil ist eine Frage der Moral. Essays zur literarischen Gesellschaftskritik der Jahrhundertwende,* edited by Peter Schmid and Tim Krohn (Zürich: 1999), pp. 157–65 (p. 164).

36 Werner Kohlschmidt, 'Der Zeitgeist in Gottfried Kellers "Martin Salander"', *Orbis Litterarum,* 22 (1967), 93–100 (100).

37 L'arte è il luogotenente dell'utopia', quoted by Hagen, p. 97.

FABIENNE REGARD

Jewish Refugees in Switzerland during the Second World War

In December 1999 the Bergier Commission's report on the treatment of refugees in Switzerland provided the general public with an official version which more or less questioned the myth of Switzerland as a haven. Does this represent an opportunity to engage in a period of mourning or alternatively bring it to an end? Is this a beginning or an end after all the upheavals the country has experienced? Although very few new facts were published, the perspective adopted was innovative; indeed, the tone changed and for the first time history was written from the point of view of the victims, no longer simply reflecting the view which had dominated since 1945.

There were three reasons why I was keen to write about the impact these events had on the collective memory. First of all, it seemed to me that the perception of the serious identity crisis which Switzerland has been experiencing since 1995 needed to be put into a historical perspective which was free of the often outrageous simplifications peddled in the media. In addition, publishing an article in English on this topic struck me as the perfect opportunity to question the Manichaean view presented on British TV by Channel Four's film on Switzerland during the War. However, one cannot be too careful in this area and it is important not to become guilty of the mistakes one criticises in others: the film in question may have been an exception and may not have represented the current state of opinion in Great Britain about Switzerland's role during the War, but the fact is that this is the way it was interpreted by a section of the Swiss population. The interplay of reflections is complex: is this the way in which the British see Switzerland or is it the way the Swiss perceive the British view of Switzerland during the Second World War? This particular aspect, although in itself worthy of further study, will not be discussed here.

Finally, and most importantly, it seems to me that when the theme of the Second World War in Switzerland is studied, it is rare for Swiss and non-Swiss Jewish testimonies to be set alongside one another and compared. In 1985 I began work on a PhD thesis on the wartime memories of Jews who were refugees in Switzerland, work which involved interviewing about 200 witnesses, and in 1997 I began collecting testimonies from 500 people of both sexes and various ages, who lived through the period of Mobilisation. This information received from those who experienced the War in Switzerland provides a better understanding of their lives at the time but above all, it gives some insight into their perceptions of and reactions to the crisis which began in 1995.

In order to clarify for the reader the facts upon which each individual's point of view is based, I will begin by outlining the legal framework in place in Switzerland with regard to refugees. I will then discuss the different types of memories recalled by Jewish refugees before finally highlighting the contradictions between individual recollections.

Reception of Refugees in Switzerland

It was often the arrival in Switzerland which contributed to the first vision of Switzerland either as a haven or on the other hand a 'little island of selfishness'. Before the War, most refugees knew Switzerland or had heard about it and had mental images of stereotypes such as an idyllic land, with snow-covered or sunny mountains, a holiday destination, a Garden of Eden (where milk, honey and chocolate were abundant). Before 1939 some had been lucky enough to visit Switzerland as tourists or students. Even if this argument does not figure largely in current historiography and even if the geostrategic situation did not leave refugees with many other options, it still seems to me that the stereotypical image of Switzerland was a decisive factor in determining refugees' expectations. However, when those who had been tourists prior to 1933 looked to the Garden of Eden to save them, Switzerland did not welcome with open arms the 'fugitives' (the term used at the time) flocking to its borders.

a. *The Laws in Existence*

Before the War the Swiss authorities took two decisions which were to have serious consequences. Following Hitler's rise to power and the first anti-Jewish measures (such as the boycott of Jewish businesses), a first wave of refugees arrived on the Swiss borders. On 7 April 1933 however, Jewish refugees were explicitly excluded from being accorded the status of political refugee.[1] This distinction remained in place until 12 July 1944 and political refugees were accepted without any problem between 1933 and 1945.

At the end of September 1938, given that Germany was employing all possible means of excluding Jews from the country's economic, political and social life, and was seeking to persuade them to emigrate, Switzerland sought to put a stop to the flood of refugees who were managing to enter the country illegally (often helped by the Gestapo). With this in mind, the Swiss proposed (via their legation in Berlin) to stamp a 'J' on the passports of all German and Austrian Jews so that they could be easily identified.[2]

Before the War, Switzerland wanted to be nothing more than a country through which refugees passed on their way to somewhere else and emigrants thus received a permit allowing them to stay only for a short time and prepare their onward journey. Under no circumstances were they allowed to work since there was a fear of foreign competition at a time of high unemployment engendered by the 1929 crash. As the situation for Jews in Germany got steadily worse (antisemitic measures, the *Anschluss*, *Kristallnacht*) and the international community failed to act (failure of the Evian Conference on Refugees and of the London Conference in 1938), several waves of refugees arrived on the Swiss borders. However, when war broke out in 1939 there were only 10,000 refugees in Switzerland.

On 5 September 1939 visas became compulsory and all foreigners had to report to the police within 24 hours of their arrival. On 17 October 1939 cantons were asked to turn back any foreigners (except for political refugees and deserters) who had arrived in Switzerland without a visa after

1   Decree of the Swiss Government, 7 April 1933.
2   Circular sent to Swiss legations and consulates by the Federal Department of Justice and Police on 4 October 1938. Austrian passports had by now been replaced by German ones and their bearers did not require a visa to enter Switzerland.

5 September.[3] Between autumn 1940 and spring 1942 few Jewish refugees attempted to enter Switzerland and thus relatively few were turned back, but in spring 1942 the Nazis started to deport Jews to Eastern Europe and many German, Dutch, Belgian and (especially after July 1942) French Jews tried to cross the border. Reception, transit and work camps were set up very quickly and as there was not enough room for everyone, prisons were also used, hotels were requisitioned and temporary accommodation built. On 4 August 1942 Rothmund, Head of Immigration, demanded that the decree of 17 October 1939 should be more strictly applied and that civilian refugees should be turned back more often, even if this might have serious consequences for them, such as loss of life.[4] The situation worsened once deportations began in France and on 13 August 1942 Rothmund ordered that the border be closed. This led to public protests and on 26 September instructions were given by phone indicating that certain categories of refugee (sick or pregnant women, those over 65 or under 16, those with family in Switzerland) should not be turned back. However, this relaxation of the rules was shortlived as on 29 December 1942 the Police Department issued very precise instructions about which illegal immigrants should be accepted. These instructions repeated that those who claimed to be refugees on the grounds of race should not be considered political refugees and, contrary to what had been decided at the end of October, they should thus be denied entry. The darkest period, during which the highest number of refugees were turned back, was from August 1942 to spring 1943.

In 1944 it started to become evident that Germany might not necessarily win the war and although the administrative instructions issued on 29 December 1942 remained officially in place, in practice attitudes were more flexible. Finally, on 12 July 1944 the instructions were changed and any refugee who feared for his or her life was considered to be a political refugee. In 1945 Switzerland went further and the government accepted 14,000 Hungarian Jews whom an SS Commander proposed to exchange for either money or goods. In addition, Jean-Marie Musy, a former member of the government, tried to negociate the liberation of Jews who had been

3   Decree issued by the Swiss government on 17 October 1939.
4   Decree issued by the Swiss government on 4 August 1942.

imprisoned in concentration camps and on 8 February 1945 1,200 survivors arrived from Theresienstadt.

During the War Switzerland took in approximately 300,000 people, including 28,000 Jews, 100,000 soldiers, 55,000 civilians, 60,000 children, 251 political refugees and 10,000 emigrants. No precise figures are available for the number turned back at the border since formalities were often dispensed with, those who did not meet the criteria for acceptance might be counted several times or not at all and some people heading for Switzerland changed their minds when they heard that the border had been closed. In addition, from 1944 onwards some Jews who could not get used to life in a camp or who did not like the idea of having an 'easy life', asked to be deported so that they could join the Resistance or go back to the place they had lived before the War. It is estimated, however, that approximately 20,000 people were refused entry to Switzerland. At the end of the War, since Switzerland was only considered to be a place of transit, Jewish refugees either returned to the country from which they had fled or emigrated to Palestine.

b. *Rewriting memories*

After the War everyone wanted things to return to normal. People wanted to live again after five years of mobilisation for Swiss soldiers, the separation of families, material and emotional deprivation, and the interruption of studies or work. When the refugees returned home they were confronted with the stark reality of the gas chambers and they had to come to terms with the fact that they would be reunited with some members of their family but not others and that they would wait for a long time for some who would never return. They also had to live with those who had been their torturers, get back their possessions which had often been stolen and continue to resist the 'Final Solution' by not dying in the immense graveyard which Europe had turned into, and at the same time become gradually more aware of the extent of the Shoah.

One point which refugees and Swiss shared just after the War was the immense, unspoken desire for normality. Indeed, by considering the phase of fundamental abnormality constituted by the Nazi counterworld as a sort of parenthesis, it was possible to get back to living, and this was a strange period during which memories cristallised, agreements were reached quickly (for example the Washington Agreements in 1946) and much remained unsaid. However, remaining silent does not mean that one forgets.

Collective Swiss memories

The fact that refugees were turned back was not spoken about after the War and the myth of Switzerland as a haven developed, helped abroad by the film made by Praesens Films, *La dernière chance* (1945), which was shown in countless Swiss embassies.[5] From time to time lone voices disagreed with the majority view but they were heavily outnumbered. In 1957, however, Carl Ludwig, a legal expert from Basel, was asked by the Swiss government to undertake a study of the federal decrees and laws which applied to refugees.[6] His work was fundamental as he had access to all the sources available which had not been destroyed and this report enabled a restricted section of the population to discover how Switzerland had treated the refugees. As for the rest of the population, they continued to believe in the myths, convinced that they had suffered during the period of Mobilisation, had preserved Switzerland from German invasion and had saved thousands of refugees. Up until 1957 the interpretations given by historians were generally favourable towards Switzerland[7] but after the publication of the Ludwig Report some became critical and emphasised three main points: many were turned back at the border, the treatment meted out in the camps was not always very welcoming and of the 300,000 refugees finally accepted, only 28,000 were Jewish, despite the fact that they constituted the most vulnerable group in the face of Nazism.[8]

---

5   See Floriane Closuit, 'La dernière chance', (Université de Lausanne, Mémoire de Licence, 1995).

6   Carl Ludwig, *La politique pratiqée par la Suisse à l'égard des réfugiés au cours des années 1933 à 1955. Rapport adressé au Conseil Fédéral à l'intention des conseils législatifs par le Professeur Carl Ludwig* (Basel: 1957).

7   See for example Robert Ginesy, *La seconde guerre mondiale et les déplacements de population* (Paris: 1948) and Jacques Vernant, *Les réfugiés dans l'après-guerre* (Monaco: 1953).

8   See for example Daniel Bourgeois, *Le Troisième Reich et la Suisse 1933–1941* (Neuchâtel: 1974); Michael Marrus, *The Unwanted European Refugees in the*

Others tended to relativise criticism and asked that there should be a more complex view of reality.[9] They emphasised Switzerland's geostrategic situation as a country with no raw materials which was surrounded by the Axis forces. How could this small nation have stood up to and provoked the Germanic boa constrictor by protecting the very Jews the Nazi regime wanted to exterminate as of 1942? Why should Switzerland have been expected to behave better than other countries, such as the United States, which were strategically less exposed (and who also failed to find solutions, as for example at Evian in 1938)? Why was it wrong for Switzerland to put her national interests first and why should she have welcomed refugees when other countries were not doing so? These two tendencies coexisted until 1995 in collective 'academic' memories in Switzerland; in politics, the dominant view was one of a neutral Switzerland, beyond reproach.

Collective memories of Jewish refugees in Switzerland

As far as collective Jewish memories are concerned, the testimonies recorded during the work done for my PhD thesis fall into three main categories, although it is important to indicate that all the refugees are grateful to Switzerland for helping them survive, even though they are sometimes very critical.[10]

Various factors, which go beyond the experiences of refugees in Switzerland, determined their interpretation of the way they were treated: age, social class, membership of youth movements, the fact of having lost their family or not, political or religious involvement or family responsibilities – all had an influence. In addition, the circumstances in which the border was crossed, the reception received, the different kinds

---

Twentieth Century (London: 1985); Walter Laqueur, *Breaking the Silence* (New York: 1986); Werner Rings, *La Suisse et la guerre 1933–1945* (Lausanne: 1975).

9   See for example Jean-Claude Favez, *Nouvelle Histoire de la Suisse et des Suisses* (Lausanne: 1983); Alfred Haesler, *La Suisse terre d'asile* (Zurich: 1971 and 1992); Ladislas Mysyrowicz, 'Le Docteur Rothmund et le problème suisse', *Revue suisse d'histoire* (1982), 348–355 and 561–562; Urs Schwarz, *The Eyes of the Hurricane: Switzerland in World War Two* (Colorado: 1980).

10   Fabienne Regard, *Les réfugiés juifs en Suisse pendant la deuxième guerre mondiale vus par le prisme de leur(s) mémoire(s)* (Forthcoming).

of camps, relations with the local population, soldiers, officials and other refugees all contributed to the establishment of a negative, positive or mixed perception. The considerable latitude accorded to camp directors explains in part why the conditions encountered by refugees in Switzerland were so variable; this can be illustrated by two extreme examples, Davesco near Lugano and Büren an der Aare.

At the camp in Davesco, about a hundred young people lived in a spacious house with rooms which each accommodated five or six people. The centre, described by its inhabitants as a 'paradise', was organised around two central aspects. In the morning there was community work, such as the clearing of a plot of land near the castle so that the camp could be self-sufficient in vegetables, agricultural work (harvesting of corn for example) and the construction of a bridge and road to improve access to a valley. In the afternoon there would be studying, and intellectual life was very active, with the refugees themselves giving talks or organising discussion groups on topics such as the finality of history or the responsibility of the German people. All those who lived at the Davesco camp emphasise the intensity of their lives there, not just as far as the official activities were concerned, but also with regard to the ideological discussions and the internal talks organised by a clandestine Communist group which enthusiastically followed world events.[11] Through contacts with Communist families in the Ticino they were often invited into Swiss homes on their trips out of the camp every six weeks. Leisure activities were just as varied and included swimming in Lake Lugano and in a nearby river, practical activities (frescoes were painted in the dining room for example), music, theatre (puppet theatre and plays by Steinbeck). There were some public performances in one of Lugano's big hotels.

However, in spite of all these positive points, it would be wrong to idealise life in this camp, where there were also hunger strikes because the food was inadequate in both quality and quantity and where there were tensions with the Director who was not used to instructing intellectuals to undertake manual activities.

---

11   Interviews with M. Spe, M. Mi, M.S, M. Su, M. Ke, M. Rot, M. Pl, M. Fe, M. Zv
      carried out in 1989 and 1990 in Israel, Belgium, Paris and Belfort. Interview with
      M. Bi carried out in Lausanne in 1999.

As for the camp at Büren an der Aare, it was situated in the Canton of Bern, not far from the Lake of Biel/Bienne, in a damp region. The accommodation consisted of wooden shacks originally built to house a division of the Polish army which had sought refuge in Switzerland at the beginning of the war; these shacks were subsequently used for civilian refugees. The camp looked like an enormous concentration camp, sanitary conditions were terrible, there was mud all around the shacks and traces of urine everywhere whenever it snowed. Very quickly, the refugees, who slept on straw and lived thirty to a shack, were plagued by scabies, lice and other parasites. Most of the refugees suffered from cold and hunger for at one time the camp director raised pigs and kept back for his own use food intended for the refugees; following protests from refugees he was replaced. The regime was very strict and it was impossible to leave the camp without being accompanied by a Swiss soldier. Only the members of youth movements or scout groups were able to organise for themselves a pleasanter life with collective activities (theatre and kitchen rotas which were strategically important for being close to food and in the warm).[12] Inaction hung heavy and brought with it anxiety and hunger.

Beyond the enormous differences which existed between camps, the personality of each individual brings an emotional aspect to the factual elements. Indeed, I interviewed two women who were in the same camp (La Chassotte, near Fribourg) at the same time and who formed very different views of their experience.[13] An in-depth analysis of their testimony shows that, although the facts were the same in the two cases, their personal commentaries were totally different. One had looked positively on aspects which the other criticised virulently; for example, for the former, getting up at 5 a.m. sometimes during the winter and going out into the snow-covered garden in shorts for the roll-call was a good way of learning discipline, being separated from her parents in the camp was character-forming and taught her to be independent. Similarly, putting up with the limitations of communal living where there was very little to eat and not enough heating, was a lesson in flexibility, just as putting up with criticisms

---

12   Interviews with M. Pl, M. Ke, M. Fe, M. Spe, M. We, M. and Mme Po. carried out in 1989 and 1990 in Israel, Belgium, France and Switzerland. Interviews with M. Bi and M. Lev conducted in 1999 and 2000 in Switzerland.
13   Interviews with Mme Ro and Mme Zi carried out in Paris in 1989.

levelled at the refugees was a way of learning about differences in mentality, and becoming the spokesperson for the group vis-a-vis a very strict camp director was a means of increasing her self confidence.

Views of Swiss treatment of Refugees expressed by 200 people who were Refugees in Switzerland 1939-1945

	positive perception	negative perception	mixed perception
no comment	A/ Survivors' syndrome	A/ Scared to say too much	This is the category into which most people fall but the sample is not representative. Like all societies Switzerland has examples of both exceptional and unacceptable behaviour
diachronic evolution	B/ At the time nothing was known about the 'Final Solution', so it was acceptable to be happy in Switzerland	B/ At the time nothing was known about the 'Final Solution'. Then the interpretation became more positive. The expression characteristic of this category is 'at that time we thought we were unfortunate but with hindsight we were really privileged'	
	C/ When the meaning of the Shoah became clear the interpretation became less positive, for the policy of turning people away at the border took on a new significance	C/ What was happening elsewhere justifies nothing, certainly not the antisemitism and xenophobia suffered in Switzerland	

It should be noted that positive comments came essentially from those who lived in camps which had an ideological basis (Communist, Zionist or religious), such as those at Versoix near Geneva or Davesco near Lugano. The very particular atmosphere of such camps also explains the enthusiasm of young people (who had sometimes lost their entire family) for a coherent, protective structure which promised a fairer future. After the War these people were happy to go back to the places in Switzerland where they had lived and to show them to their families and they sent their children to Switzerland on holiday. Negative comments put the emphasis on bad food, the general atmosphere, the feeling of having been abandoned and being alone, the impression of being looked down upon as 'the poor little refugee', bad treatment, punishments and periods spent in prison. Those who figure under the classification 'negative perception C' very often refused to return to Switzerland after 1945 or did not do so until many years had gone by. Finally, the mixed perception took the view that just as social reality is complex, so there were both extraordinary individuals (generous citizens, welcoming and open towards the refugees) and others who displayed unacceptable behaviour (antisemitism and xenophobia). This perception is the one shared by most people, although the sample is not (and could never be) representative.

Since 1995

Between 1945 and 1995 memories seemed on the whole to cristallise for in reality the publication of the Ludwig Report did nothing to upset the myth in which the general public continued to believe. However, in May 1995 suddenly, following the publication in the newspapers of articles about dormant bank accounts and the fiftieth anniversary of the end of the War, the Swiss government presented a public apology for the introduction of the 'J' on passports in autumn 1938 and expressed regret for the policy of turning people away at the border. Kaspar Villiger, the Swiss President, declared that 'I am in no doubt that as far as our policy towards the persecuted Jews is concerned, we were guilty. The fear of Germany, the fear that there would be too many foreigners if a massive number of immigrants were accepted, and the fear of encouraging latent antisemitism here, weighed more heavily than our tradition of asylum and our humanitarian traditions.'[14] At the request of the Jewish organisation Yad Vashem, research on the numbers of refugees turned back at the border had begun some years earlier in the federal archives in Bern. The process seemed to have been set in motion, cracks began to appear in the established picture of the Second World War, cracks which were followed by the sounds of chains being broken, as others shouted that it was scandalous and unfair.

Everything changed definitively and it became impossible to go backwards. The tone was set, television programmes accused, violently and disrespectfully denounced a selfish Switzerland which had profited from the War and was antisemitic. 'Politically correct' views were turned upside down, these new critics were taken to court, those who had been mobilised during the War had no idea what on earth was happening with this *coup d'état* on their memories. The young demanded explanations, as if it was vital at all costs to get the question sorted out with the generation that had experienced the War, so that the burden could be laid down. Communication was impossible.

The titles of works published since this date speak volumes about the vision of Switzerland which they contain.[15] The tone became heated, things which had never been said came out into the open, a politician of the calibre of Jean-Pascal Delamuraz, member of the government, made an antisemitic remark in *La Tribune de Genève* (31 December 1996) and it was the beginning of the end of silence. Passions ran high in the correspondence pages of newspapers and antisemitism came out into the open once again. Was this the beginning of a process or the end of a myth? Collective Jewish memories were not spared either for how should you react if you were given refuge by Switzerland during the War and saved? The positive comments made about Switzerland were revisited, the

14 Declaration by Kaspar Villiger, 7 May 1995.
15 For example Anne Weill-Levy et al, *Un essai sur le racisme d'état (1900–1942)* (Lausanne: 1999); Daniel Bourgeois, *Business helvétique et Troisième Reich* (Lausanne: 1998); Hans Ulrich Jost, *Le salaire des neutres. Suisse 1938–1948* (Paris: 1999); Yael and Pierre Hazan, *La Suisse des bons sentiments. Voyage en terre d'asile* (Genève: 1996); Adam Lebor, *Hitler's Secret Bankers. The Myth of Swiss Neutrality during the Holocaust* (Secaucus/New Jersey: 1997); Tom Bower, *Nazi Gold. The Full Story of the Fifty-Year Swiss-Nazi Conspiracy to steal Billions from Europe's Jews and Holocaust Survivors* (New York: 1997).

gratitude of many was noted and it was suggested that the names of those given refuge should be published. Isn't there a risk that the 'survivors' syndrome', discernable in some testimonies before 1995, will as a result be accentuated?

Conclusion

The drastic re-evaluation of memories was doubtless made possible by various factors whose precise value cannot be determined very easily: there was thus a demographic factor, the arrival of new generations who wielded a certain power over public opinion (the political world as well as the media, researchers and teachers), the progressive disappearance of some of those who lived through the War and external pressure from international public opinion with a potential economic impact through the boycott of Swiss banks, for example. Faced with these changes, those who experienced the War are still not sure how to fight back: should they speak out and try to convince people that 'we did what we could with what we had and with what we were' or keep quiet and take refuge behind slogans such as 'you young people weren't in the War, you don't understand anything, you know nothing about the context, we're doubly victimised, firstly because of Mobilisation which stole our youth and secondly because of the memories to which we are sacrificing our honour and our old age'? Many of those concerned seem to have chosen the second tactic and have decided to remain silent. Unfortunately, they no longer have 50 years ahead of them during which to express their point of view.

The controversy surrounding Switzerland's past and her attitude towards Jewish refugees will at least have had the merit of expanding knowledge of this period in several areas. It has brought about a more qualified view of relations between refugees and Swiss, a more precise awareness of the prejudices towards Jews and foreigners which existed and an understanding of the social and economic situation of those who were mobilised and their families. In fact, after moving from the idyllic myth of a haven to the anti-myth of the country which profited from the War, the next stage will perhaps make it possible to reach a fairer, less simplistic view which does not see the world in black and white. Not all Swiss were antisemitic, but some people who lived through the War often express virulently antisemitic opinions. Not all Swiss were against the refugees, but it would be wrong to separate an inhuman official policy from a mainly welcoming Swiss population. If the Swiss did not wish to accept the official line, they did not necessarily have to and each time there were demonstrations against the closure of the border (in 1938 and again in 1942) the government took account of people's views. Life in the camps was nothing like the life the refugees had had before the War but was it anything like the daily life experienced by those who had been mobilised? In material terms perhaps it was similar but we must not forget that the refugees were persecuted, they feared for their lives and they had had to leave their homelands and be imprisoned in camps in the name of state interests which they did not understand. It is indeed not always possible to explain why certain camp directors failed to see and recognise the human beings who were under their protection and only saw in them the means of exercising arbitrary power. Being given responsibility for a sizeable group of people went to the heads of some ordinary individuals who as a consequence became unbearable and abused their position. Caught in a situation which was neither black nor white, mobilised Switzerland was in military grey.

Translated by Joy Charnley

BRIGITTE SCHNEGG

Looking back to the Future: Designs for an Ideal Society in the Swiss Enlightenment

The Enlightenment was characterised, like other ages of re-orientation and transition, by tension between the present and the future, between what is given and what is desirable, between the factual and the Utopian. Enlightenment thinking claimed to examine thoroughly the legitimacy of the existing situation and to subject traditional notions and certainties to systematic criticism.[1] The present was seen as consisting of problems arising from a situation of crisis from which society had to emerge with the help of enlightenment and reform. 'Criticism' and 'crisis' are thus the two key concepts under which Reinhard Kosellek subsumes the movement of the Enlightenment and from which he derives the revolutionary dynamism of the Enlightenment.[2] Ranged against them are the contrary concepts of 'reform' and 'Utopia' used by Francesco Venturi to characterise the Enlightenment,[3] two terms which, as Ulrich Im Hof has shown, correspond in the German language of the Enlightenment to 'improvement' and 'dreams'.[4] 'Criticism' and 'crisis', 'reform' and 'Utopia', 'dreams' and 'improvements' are therefore the key terms which set the parameters within which Enlightenment thought and action developed in the eighteenth century. They stand for a critical inventory of the existing situation as well as for the future-oriented possibilities for action and visions of the *philosophes* of the eighteenth century, who were both theorists and practical men, thinkers and politicians, scholars, ministers of religion or pedagogues, merchants, farmers or statesmen.

1   Horst Möller, *Vernunft und Kritik. Die deutsche Aufklärung im 17. und 18. Jahrhundert* (Frankfurt am Main: 1986).
2   Reinhard Kosellek, *Kritik und Krise. Eine Studie zur Pathogenese der bürgerlichen Welt* (Frankfurt am Main: 1973).
3   Franco Venturi, *Utopia e Riforma nell'Illuminismo* (Turin: 1970).
4   Ulrich Im Hof, *Das Europa der Aufklärung* (Munich: 1993), p. 134.

The dream of a better world was also dreamt by the Swiss representatives of the Enlightenment. In 1755, young Isaak Iselin (1728–1782) from Basel published his *Filosofische und patriotische Träume eines Menschenfreundes*,[5] which during his lifetime went to several editions and revised versions.[6] In 1758 the same Isaak Iselin published *Patriotische Träume eines Eidgenossen von einem Mittel, die veraltete Eidgenossenschaft wieder zu verjüngen*, which the Luzern patrician and city councillor Franz Urs Balthasar had already written in 1744 but had not dared to publish.[7]

In this essay, I will draw on these two texts as well as on the general discourse to describe the Swiss Enlightenment's search for the ideal social structure. This search is conditioned to a great extent by the fact that the Swiss city-states and country cantons of the eighteenth century were, in contrast to most of their European neighbours, constituted as republics or democracies. The representatives of the Enlightenment, apart from a few exceptions, attributed great political and ethical value to a republican constitution which was associated with the idea of the freedom of the citizen, even if they often sharply criticised the political reality of their respective cantons. Their criticism, however, was directed not at the republican constitution as such but what it had become, at the tendency towards oligarchical monopolisation of power, for example, at the inability to enact practical reforms, at despotism or corruption by representatives of the authorities.[8] In view of these abuses, which were interpreted as signs of decadence, the Enlightenment thinkers searched through history for models on which a future order of society might be oriented. The dialectic

---

5   Isaak Iselin, *Filosofische und Patriotische Träume eines Menschenfreundes* (Freiburg: 1755).

6   *Philosophische und Patriotische Träume eines Menschenfreundes*, second expanded edition (Zürich: 1762), *Philosophische und Patriotische Träume eines Menschenfreundes*, third expanded edition (Zürich: 1776); finally a fourth edition appeared in Karlsruhe under the title *Träume eines Menschenfreundes* in 1784 after Iselin's death.

7   The text appeared anonymously, (Franz Urs Balthasar), *Patriotische Träume eines Eydgnossen von einem Mittel die veraltete Eydgnoßschaft wieder zu verjüngeren*, Freystadt bei Wilhelm Tells Erben, 1758 (Lörrach: 1758).

8   There were also critics from time to time, e.g. Johann Heinrich Pestalozzi, for example, who, on account of the political paralysis of the Swiss republics, flirted with the political form of enlightened monarchy in which they saw a better realisation of reforms. But these supporters of enlightened monarchy will not be discussed here.

of past and future, of social criticism and visions of the future which marks these backward-looking designs for a society of the future is at the centre of this essay.

However different the two 'dreams' and their inventors Isaak Iselin and Franz Urs Balthasar were, they both testify to a widespread feeling in the eighteenth century that the prevailing political, social or moral conditions were wanting and in need of improvement. After intensive study of political theory and as a counter to the political situation in his home town, Iselin drew up an ideal political order based on the premisses of natural law,[9] whereas Balthasar, convinced of the necessity for reform in his country on the basis of his political experience in the old Confederation, dreamed of a confederal institution of education for young men in which the future elites of the Swiss republics were to be imbued with the capabilities, knowledge and virtues necessary for their functions and in which unity and friendship amongst members of the Confederation were to be promoted and strengthened.[10]

The two Utopias, the political and the pedagogic, not only shared an implicit criticism of current conditions. Utopian thinking, by relating critically to the present and at the same time hopefully to the future, is also always historical and philosophical since it contains an idea of the course of history. The present and the future are placed in a line of development that is seen from the point of view of progress or of decline; present and future are either contrasted with a less developed, darker period of history or with a past golden age.

So it was not by chance that in the Swiss Enlightenment a preoccupation with the future was accompanied by an intensive study of history. Thus, after his *Philosophische und patriotische Träume*, Isaak Iselin in 1764 published his *Philosophische Muthmassungen über die Geschichte*, a history of the evolution of mankind and human civilisation from the

---

9   Iselin had engaged with the Ancient Greeks, for example with Plato, just as intensively as with contemporary authors, such as Montesquieu or Christian Wolff; on Iselin's 'Träume' see Ulrich Im Hof, *Isaak Iselin. Sein Leben und die Entwicklung seines Denkens bis zur Abfassung der 'Geschichte der Menschheit' von 1764* (Basel: 1947), pp. 371–88.

10   On Franz Urs Balthasar and his 'Patriotische Träume', see Ulrich Im Hof, *Aufklärung in der Schweiz* (Bern: 1970), pp. 44–46.

'natural state' to the present.[11] This text was to a great extent a counter-model to the theory of history presented by another Swiss, namely, to Jean-Jacques Rousseau's concept of a state of nature which he had developed in his *Discours sur les sciences et les arts* (1750) and his *Discours sur l'origine et les fondements de l'inégalité parmi les hommes* (1754). In contradistinction to Leibniz's disciple Iselin, Rousseau espoused a pessimistic view of the future that was critical of society since he saw the development of mankind moving ever further away from the ideal condition of the Golden Age. In Rousseau's eyes, civilisation did not represent progress, but rather a process of alienation and moral decline.

Besides Iselin and Rousseau, many other representatives of the Swiss Enlightenment also concerned themselves intensively with history. Johann Jakob Bodmer, Professor of National History at the Carolineum in Zürich, collected source material on the history of Zürich and the Confederation, wrote historical dramas and successfully encouraged his students to study the past. Many of the leading figures conducted historical research, collected historical documents or even wrote historical treatises. The study of national history occurs again and again in the stated aims of Enlightenment societies.[12] In the Swiss Enlightenment, history was a major point of orientation in the discussion of the present and in the designs for the future.

The consideration of the past of course took very different forms with different authors. Thus, Isaak Iselin rejected the notion of an ideal state of nature in the past. He saw the golden age before him, in the future. Franz Urs Balthasar, on the other hand, evoked an ideal past within one's own history which was transfigured into myth and which provided a model for the present and the future. For him, as for many representatives of the Swiss Enlightenment, the heroic age was situated in the historical context of one's own past, in the Switzerland of his forefathers. The founding period of the

---

11   Compare Ulrich Im Hof, *Isaak Iselin und die Spätaufklärung* (Bern: 1967), pp. 77–100.

12   In particular the two societies concerned with history and politics initiated by Bodmer, the 'Gesellschaft zur Gerwi' and the 'Gesellschaft zu Schumachern', placed great importance on the study of national history. But other societies, such as the 'Berner Gesellschaft Patriotischer Freunde' also aimed to support their own political education by nurturing the 'history of our free state'. See Emil Erne, *Die schweizerischen Sozietäten. Lexikalische Darstellung der Reformgesellschaften des 18. Jahrhunderts in der Schweiz* (Zürich: 1988).

old Confederation and the age of conflict with feudal lords especially were held to be the heroic age of Swiss history.

Iselin on the one side, and Balthasar along with a large number of the representatives of the Swiss Enlightenment on the other, also differed in their assessment of the course history was taking. Whereas Iselin – in contrast to Rousseau – assumed a progressive development proceeding positively, the present appeared to those holding a critical view of society as an era of decadence:

> Und, was uns mit Forcht und Schrecken überhäufen sol, ist, daß wir sehen, wie unser geliebtes Vaterland auf eben dieser Strasse dem Untergang zuwandert, ohne daß, auch sonst eifrige Patrioten mit Ueberlegungen bemühen, wie doch dem drohenden Uebel vorgebogen werden möge.[13]

Thus lamented Franz Urs Balthasar, for example, who saw a possible way out of the threatening situation by reflecting on the 'guten Sitten, nutzlichen Gebräuche, und herrlichen Tathen (der) Voreltern'; 'nach zurückgeführter Tugend, Beobachtung der Gesetz- und Ordnungen', his hope was that 'in kurzer Frist der Jahre, das Vaterland in ehvorigem Stand, Flor und Ansehen' would be restored.[14]

A generation later, Johann Kaspar Lavater, the young theologian from Zürich and a student of Johann Jakob Bodmer, evoked the decline of his country: 'Ach! Sinken seh' ich dich – seh' deine Hoheit fallen', he cried in *Zuruf des Schweizerliederdichters an sein Vaterland*, and continued: 'O könnt allhörbar noch in dir mein Ruf erschallen/ Mein Ruf! Sey was du warst!...'[15] Like Balthasar, in whose *Träume* the 'ehvorige Stand' provided the point of orientation, Lavater also referred to former conditions in the heroic past, more precisely to the virtues of the forefathers: 'Wo ist die alte Kraft? Wo ist das unentnerfte,/ das knochigte Geschlecht? Wo – eine Heldenschaar?/ Wo ist der starke Sinn, den Noth und Freyheit schärfte?/ Wo Mann und Männin noch – wo Held und Heldin war,' he asked, and

13 (Franz Urs Balthasar), 'Patriotische Träume eines Eydgnossen von einem Mittel die veraltete Eydgnoßschaft wieder zu verjüngeren', in *Verhandlungen der Helvetischen Gesellschaft 1765*, p. 17.
14 ibid, p. 18f.
15 Johann Kaspar Lavater, *Schweizer Lieder*, 4th improved and expanded edition (Zürich: 1775), p. 180.

concluded anxiously that 'die Kunst der Weichlichkeit zerstampfet jede Spur von reinem Schweizersinn, von Würde, von Natur'.[16] Johann Kaspar Lavater wrote his *Schweizer Lieder* at the instigation of the 'Helvetische Gesellschaft',[17] which hoped in this way to popularise its patriotic ideals. It was Martin von Planta, an aristocrat from the Grisons, who, at the meeting of 1766, proposed the creation of just such a collection of songs. His aim was 'zur Erweckung tugendhafter und grossmüthiger Gesinnungen bey dem Landvolk, die besten Thaten unserer Väter in einfaltigen Liedern lebhaft vorzustellen'.[18] Songs that praised the heroism and virtue of the forefathers were to hold up models to those contemporaries incapable of reading and to contribute to the moral education of the rural population. They should promote a moral regeneration of the Swiss people by recalling the old ideals of virtue. Just a year later, Lavater published a first collection of songs which, in manifold variations, praised the purity of the morals of the Ancients and the heroic past of Switzerland.[19] The *Schweizer Lieder* had enormous success, so that further editions very soon followed which were in part revised and enlarged.[20] For Lavater, who as a student had enthusiastically attended the lectures of Bodmer on national history, the moral order of the past was the orientation point for this renewal of his

16   ibid, p. 181f.
17   The 'Helvetische Gesellschaft' was founded in 1762 by Isaak Iselin, Salomon Hirzel and Salomon Gessner with the aim 'Freundschaft und Liebe, Verbindung und Eintracht unter den Eidgenossen zu stiften und zu erhalten, die Triebe zu schönen, guten und edlen Thaten auszubreiten, und Friede, Freyheit und Tugend, durch die Freunde des Vaterlandes auf künftige Alter und Zeiten fortzupflanzen'. The society comprised a large number of the leading personalities of the Swiss Enlightenment and met annually in a session lasting several days. See for details Ulrich Im Hof, *Das Entstehen einer politischen Öffentlichkeit in der Schweiz* (*Die Helvetische Gesellschaft. Spätaufklärung und Vorrevolution in der Schweiz*, vol 1) (Frauenfeld/ Stuttgart: 1983).
18   *Verhandlungen der Helvetischen Gesellschaft 1766*, p. 10, quoted by Im Hof, *Helvetische Gesellschaft*, p. 199.
19   The first edition of the *Schweizer Lieder*, published in 1767, contained amongst other things nine actual battle songs, which evoked the heroism of the Swiss warriors at the medieval battles of Morgarten, Sempach, Näfels, Laupen, St Jakob an der Birs, etc.
20   On the *Schweizer Lieder* and the history of their creation and publication, see Im Hof, *Helvetische Gesellschaft*, pp. 199–204.

own society. In this regard he was largely in agreement with his famous teacher and friends in Zürich. The Enlightenment in Zürich, as influenced by Bodmer along with many members of the 'Helvetische Gesellschaft', saw in the preoccupation with history a source of edification and an effective means of promoting the moral education of their contemporaries.

How they imagined the pedagogic effect of history is shown by the speech of Urs Joseph Glutz from Solothurn to the 'Helvetische Gesellschaft' in 1787 which reminded its listeners of the demise of the Greek republics and derived from this a call for moral reforms:

> So fiel Sparta, so fiel Athen, so fiel Rom. O möchte doch jeder Helvetier auf den Trümmern dieser ehemals so berühmten Staaten die heilsame Wahrheit lesen, dass kein Freystaat ohne gute Sitten und ohne Tugend in die Länge bestehen könnte.[21]

If Lavater mainly took the positive model of heroic forefathers from history, Glutz here pointed to the deterrent of the historic example of the republics of the Ancients, from whose collapse the republics of the Confederation ought to draw lessons. In the historical discourse of the Swiss Enlightenment, this connection was also often evoked. For the representatives of the Enlightenment, schooled in the classical authors, but also in Montesquieu, the republics of Greek and Roman antiquity were extremely instructive examples, especially since the problem of decadence and decline, with which they were intensely concerned, could be very well studied in them. In addition, because of their republican constitution, the states of the ancient world seemed particularly well suited for a comparison with the cantons of the Confederation. This relationship between the two was emphasised for example by the Appenzell doctor and friend of Bodmer Laurenz Zellweger, when he thought about the causes of the decline of the Greek city-states:

> Die Griechischen Republicken [...] welche die meiste Conformität mit unsern Schweizerischen Republicken haben, geben uns [...] genugsamen Beweisthum und Exempel an die Hand. Denn da sie durch ihre Tapferkeit und kluges einmüthiges Betragen sich in Ruhe und Wohlstand gesetzet, die Gesetze beobachtet, Künste und Wissenschaften

---

21 *Verhandlungen der Helvetischen Gesellschaft 1787*, p. 36, quoted by Im Hof, *Helvetische Gesellschaft*, p. 181.

florieren gemachet und bey öftern freundschaftlichen Zusammenkünften in den olympischen und andern Spielen wegen Geistes- und Leibes-Übungen um die Wette gestritten ec., so lebten sie glücklich und in Ruhe und Frieden; so bald aber das Misstrauen, die Herrsch- und Habsucht, der Luxus, der Müssiggang, die Leichtsinnigkeit, die Verachtung der alten Fondamental-Gesetze, Recht und Gebräuche, und eine gänzliche Verdorbenheit der Sitten eingerissen, so sind die Republicken unter sich selbsten in Uneinigkeit und eine nach der andern in Verfall gerathen und zuletzt alle von fremden Mächten unterjocht worden.[22]

With his depiction of the flourishing and the decline of the Greek republics, Zellweger was basically drafting a positive as well as a negative scenario for the social and political development of his country. In the portrayal of the well-ordered Greek society prior to its decline, the outlines of an ideal and social and political order become visible: calm and prosperity, peace and lawfulness, flourishing arts and sciences as well as a living culture of sociability distinguished the model community in the eyes of Zellweger. He wished Switzerland to be like that.

This harmony was threatened mainly from within, by the human weaknesses and vices of the men and women living in these peaceful republics. Only when distrust, thirst for power and greed undermined unity, only when luxury, frivolity and idleness destroyed prosperity and only when disregard of laws and traditions destroyed public order did it become possible for foreign powers to conquer and subjugate the formerly prospering republics and so to seal their decline. Amongst the representatives of the Swiss Enlightenment, there was agreement that it was the decline in virtues and morals of the citizens which was striking at the core of the republics. There was also agreement with Montesquieu's conviction that republics, as distinct from monarchies, were based on the principle of virtue,[23] and that, as a consequence, the loss of virtue was inevitably followed by the decline of the republican state. The key to a permanent and stable order with the Swiss was therefore to strengthen the morality of their citizens.

The virtue of republican citizens was, in the agreed opinion of most of the representatives of the Enlightenment in Switzerland, the basis for a

---

22 *Verhandlungen der helvetischen Gesellschaft 1764*, pp. 39–54.
23 Montesquieu, *De l'esprit des lois*, Livre III, Chap. III.

happy republic. To guarantee this, Franz Urs von Balthasar dreamed of an institute of education for the young men of the country. He earned widespread assent to this proposal.[24] The consolidation of virtue was also the more or less explicit aim of many Enlightenment societies[25] and the many moral weeklies pursued the same goal.[26] But whereas there was agreement about their fundamental political significance, opinions differed about the social and economic premisses for the development and maintenance of public virtue. Especially disputed was the question whether riches and abundance were beneficial or harmful for the virtue of the public. If many were convinced that too much prosperity led to luxury and luxury in turn to vice and idleness and so brought about the ruin of public morality, there were voices on the other hand which saw in prosperity and affluence the prerequisite for the development of moral behaviour. Albrecht von Haller, the universal scholar and doctor from Bern, was amongst those who saw the basis of virtue in a scarcity of goods. In his poem *Die Alpen*, published in 1729 and destined to become very famous, he praised the natural austerity of the populated Alpine area as a source of happiness and moral integrity of the Helvetic Alpine peoples:

> Wohl dir, vergnügtes Volk! O danke dem Geschicke/
> Das dir der Laster Quell, den Überfluss, versagt,/
> Dem, den sein Stand vergnügt, dient Armut selbst zum Glücke,/
> Da Pracht und Üppigkeit der Länder Stütze nagt.

---

24 The 'Helvetische Gesellschaft' took up his idea and attempted to realise a project for a national seminar, see Im Hof, *Die Helvetische Gesellschaft*, p. 169f. Education was additionally a central concern of the Swiss Enlightenment which brought forth a whole series of famous pedagogues, such as Johann Heinrich Pestalozzi, Ulysses von Salis and Philipp Emanual von Fellenberg.

25 This is true not only of those societies which carried this aim in their name, such as for example the moral societies, but also additionally for the patriotic and the historical or political societies some of which exercised, in internal matters too, strict control over the behaviour of their members, see Erne, op. cit. and Rolf Graber, *Bürgerliche Öffentlichkeit und spätabsolutistischer Staat. Sozietätenbewegung und Konfliktkultur in Zürich 1746–1780* (Zürich: 1993).

26 See Wolfgang Martens, *Die Botschaft der Tugend, Die Aufklärung im Spiegel der deutschen moralischen Wochenschriften* (Stuttgart: 1968).

Haller also drew the parallel with antiquity and connected the fall of Rome with the fact that riches proliferated beyond control:

> Als Rom die Siege noch bey seinen Schlachten zählte,/
> War Brei der Helden Speis, und Holz der Götter Haus;/
> Als aber ihm das Maas von seinem Reichtum fehlte,/
> Trat bald der schwächste Feind den feigen Stolz in Graus./
> Du aber hüte dich, was Grössers zu begehren./
> Solang die Einfalt dauert, wird auch der Wohlstand währen.

Absence of riches was of course for Haller not simply beneficial for virtue and a healthy way of life, since he also saw in it the guarantee of republican equality which for its part was considered to be the fundamental principle of a properly functioning republic:

> Glückseliger Verlust von schadenvollen Gütern!/
> Der Reichthum hat kein Gut, das eurer Armuth gleicht;/
> Die Eintracht wohnt bey euch in friedlichen Gemüthern,/
> Weil kein beglänzter Wahn euch Zweytrachtsäpfel reicht;/
> [...]
> Hier herrscht kein Unterschied, den schlauer Stolz erfunden,/
> Der Tugend unterthan, und Laster edel macht;[27]

Like Zellweger's picture of the Greek republics, Haller's poem on the Alps contains an ideal of society oriented towards the past. The Alpine world glorified by him, although situated in the present, corresponds in its simplicity to some extent to a situation of pre-civilisation which is praised as being pure and unspoilt. 'Beglückte güldne Zeit, Geschenk der ersten Güte,/ O dass der Himmel dich so zeitig weggerückt!'. On this lament about the loss of the Golden Age at the beginning of Haller's long poem, there follows the consoling realisation that something of the lost paradise has been retained in Alpine society:

> Ihr Schüler der Natur, ihr kennt noch güldne Zeiten!/
> Nicht zwar ein Dichterreich voll fabelhafter Pracht;/
> Wer misst den äussern Glanz scheinbarer Eitelkeiten,/
> Wann Tugend Müh zur Lust und Armut glücklich macht?[28]

---

27 Albrecht von Haller, 'Die Alpen', in Haller, *Die Alpen und andere Gedichte* (Stuttgart: 1965), pp. 5f.

28 ibid.

It is true that Haller is one of the first but by no means the only person who redefined poverty and distance from civilisation positively. A similar position was taken up later, mainly by Jean-Jacques Rousseau. The radical wing of the Swiss Enlightenment committed to the 'Citoyen de Genève' declared frugality, thrift and modesty to be the pillars of an ascetic republican canon of virtue. The anti-patrician nature of this view could not be overlooked.[29]

The counter-position to this idealisation of simplicity and scarcity was again taken up by Isaak Iselin. He was convinced that prosperity did not destroy virtue but instead made it possible. In the chapter about the moral order in *Philosophische und patriotische Träume*, he wrote:

> Ohne wirtschaftlichen Wohlstand würde das menschliche Geschlecht sich niemals zu einem beträchtlichen Grade der Tugend erhoben haben. Ohne den Feldbau und ohne die Künste würden die Menschen immer in der Wildheit und in der Unwissenheit geblieben seyn, würden sie einander immer verfolget und bekrieget haben.

And with an indirect dig at Rousseau, and probably against Haller too, he continued:

> Ein rohes, armes und unbeschäftigtes Volk kann niemals ein tugend-haftes Volk werden. Die Poeten mögen uns auch die seligen Folgen der Niedrigkeit und der Armuth noch so einnehmend abschildern, sie werden doch niemals ein glückseliges und schätzbares Volk bilden. Ein einzelner Weise kann in der Armuth und in dem Elende gross, tugendhaft und glückselig seyn; aber nicht ein ganzes Volk. Damit ein Volk tugendhaft und glücklich werden könne, muss die Gesellschaft sich in einer Art von Ueberflusse befinden. Was die Philosophen die Nahrung und den Zunder des Lasters nennen, ist auch die Nahrung und der Zunder der Tugend. In dem Müssiggange und in der Unthätigkeit, welche mit einer allgemeinen Armuth und einer durchgehenden Rohigkeit der Sitten unabänderlich verknüpfet sind, können weder die feinern Vermögen des Geistes, noch die erhabenen Gefühle des Herzens sich entwickeln. Nur nach Massgabe wie die Güter des Lebens sich vermehren, werden die Menschen aufgemuntert, ihre edlen Fähigkeiten

---

29   See Rolf Graber's comments on the confrontational culture of the Zürich members of the Enlightenment, especially pp. 47–80.

zu versuchen, und in Stand gesetzet, das Gute aus einer vernünftigen
Kenntnis zu wollen und in einem weitern Unterfangen auszuüben.[30]

Thus Isaak Iselin from the commercial city of Basel took a decidedly
different view in respect of material prosperity and its consequences from
the majority of his Enlightenment contemporaries. In his opinion, vice did
not pose a threat because of abundance, but because of poverty, lack of
activity and hopelessness deriving from material need. Iselin's theory about
the end of the natural condition is interesting in this context. Like Rousseau,
he assumed that the original condition of natural equality of all men had
been destroyed by the human drive for enjoyment, riches and power,[31] but
unlike Rousseau, he saw in the human 'Begihrde reich zu werden' a source
of energy for the further development of mankind and for the creation of a
society in which prosperity, morality and order reigned:

> Weit entfernt, dass die Vermehrung der Bedürfnisse ein Unglück für
> die Menschheit seyn sollte, wie es einige Sittenlehrer behaupten: glaube
> ich viel eher, [...] dass sie in allen Gesichtspunkten die Glückseligkeit
> des Menschen vermehre, in dem sittlichen, weil ohne dieselben er nicht
> arbeiten, und weil ohne Arbeit er nothwendig schlimm und unglücklich
> seyn würde, im wirthschaftlichen, weil durch sie die Masse der
> gesellschaftlichen Güter vermehret wird; und im politischen, weil ohne
> sie der Mensch die Würde des Bürgers nicht behaupten kann, und er
> ein Sklave oder ein Tyrann, ein Weichling oder ein Barbar seyn wird.
> Die Begihrde reich zu werden ist also als eine unumgängliche Bedingnis
> anzusehen, ohne welche weder die wirtschaftliche noch die sittliche
> Tugend sich merklich ausbreiten können. [...] Obschon also die
> Begihrde reich zu werden nicht Tugend ist, so kann doch ohne sie die
> Tugend nicht entstehen. Armuth und Mangel können, wo sie allgemein
> sind, nichts erzeugen als sittliches und wirtschaftliches Elend.[32]

The positions could not be more different between what Iselin is arguing
and the views held by Rousseau and his followers in Switzerland. Whereas
Iselin saw a comprehensive civilising force in the human drive for riches
and material abundance, a force which did not simply improve the economic
conditions of the republican community, but also influenced its moral state

---

30   Isaak Iselin, *Philosophische und patriotische Träume eines Menschenfreundes*, pp.
     224–26.
31   Isaak Iselin, *Träume II*, p. 46, and Im Hof, *Isaak Iselin*, p. 379.
32   Isaak Iselin, *Träume* (1784 edition), p. 225, p. 228.

and even its political constitution, it was precisely here, in the eyes of the members of the Enlightenment critical of society, that the root of all evil lay. For them, riches and affluence were the roads to luxury and the love of splendour. And these in their turn were the beginning of all negative developments. They corrupted personal virtue, destroyed the economic situation of families and, lastly, undermined equality, one of the political pillars of the republican social constitution.

Luxury, its causes and consequences and the fight against it, were among the most discussed topics of the Swiss Enlightenment. Speeches were made about it, debates were held, competitions organised and pamphlets written.[33] The vast majority was convinced that luxury was threatening to get the upper hand and that it therefore had to be attacked with all possible means, that sumptuary laws should limit by decree the display of splendour and that by means of an appropriate moral education the tendency to luxury should be combatted on an individual level. Here again, Iselin was one of the few who was of a different opinion, rejecting the sumptuary laws as unfit for the strengthening of public morality.

It is beyond the scope of the present essay to examine these debates further. But one aspect of this discourse may be mentioned in conclusion. Luxury was considered by the members of the Enlightenment as a vice to which the female sex was said to be especially prone. The changing habits and deportment of the upper echelons of society, which were observed in the course of the eighteenth century in the Swiss cities, the increasing distinction between urban patricians through a more lavish life-style following French models – changes which had a multiplicity of cultural, economic and social causes – were again and again attributed to female influence. Even when the import of French life-styles and articles of fashion was attributed by some to the Huguenot refugees, by others to the Swiss officers serving in French armies or to the boom in the Swiss textile industry, the real road to luxury was seen in the receptivity of women for the new forms which flattered their vanity. Thus the Vaudois pastor, Abraham Ruchat, was already in 1714 writing in his *Délices de la Suisse*: 'Anciennement les Moeurs des Suisses étoient fort simples'. But today everything was different:

---

33 On the debates about this in the 'Helvetische Gesellschaft', see Im Hof, *Helvetische Gesellschaft*, pp. 158–62.

Aujourd'hui les choses ont bien changé. Graces au service de la France, les Officiers Suisses se sont délourdis, & ont appris les belles manières. Les dames [...] les ont apprises d'eux, et les hommes se polissent auprès des Dames. Mais avec leur politesse, la franchise, la pureté, la simplicité, la frugalité et la cordialité ancienne se perdent peu-à-peu, & la dissimulation, l'hypocrisie, & le libertinage, qu'on appelle galanterie, prennent leur place.[34]

The establishment of a refined style of life is seen by the rigorously moral pastor and essayist as a collapse of morality which has been brought about by women. Numerous contemporary texts tell in similar fashion of an allegedly fateful social and cultural transformation which has been initiated by women. Thus an 'altväterischer, aber redlich denkender Patriot', in a text written in 1740 but not published until 1784 in *Schweizerisches Museum* with the significant title 'Moralische Schilderung des ehemals altfränkischen, itzt aber artigen *** Frauenzimmers', reports on the development of a refined life-style in his home town. This transformation, according to the author, behind whom none other than Franz Urs Balthasar from Luzern is hiding, has in the end brought about general economic ruin and a complete collapse of morals in his home town. He laments the fact that young women have turned away from the old domestic ideals of their mothers, from thrift, modesty and rigorous morals. The 'Frauenzimmer von dem Schrot und Korn früherer Jahrhunderte' had, according to the text, distinguished herself by seclusion and a thrifty nature and had concerned herself with 'kein anderes als die eigentlichen Hausgeschäfte'. But the 'artigen Frauenzimmer' of the new era despised the virtues of their mothers, neglected their duties and instead cultivated a social life on the French model, with conversation, dances and games. They wasted money on new, fashionable clothing, on refined interiors and opulent food and drink and led their children astray by their example to conduct a slothful life-style until finally the domestic economy was destroyed and their offspring corrupted.[35] The moral of this didactic article by Franz Urs Balthasar is obvious. The dissociation from a rigorous ancient order, from former frugality and from the rigid integration of women into domestic

---

34   Abraham Ruchat, *Les Délices de la Suisse* (Leiden: 1714), p. 777.
35   'Moralische Schilderung des ehemals altfränkischen, itzt artigen *** Frauenzimmers, von einem altväterischen, aber redlich denkenden Patrioten', in *Schweizerisches Museum 1784*, pp. 740–53.

duties led to ruin. The assumption of a refined life-style and the social mixing of the sexes associated with it was proving to be extraordinarily threatening to the republic since it undermined public morality to a dangerous degree. Accordingly, for most members of the Enlightenment, a 'polite society' on the French model in Switzerland was not an appropriate goal. Instead, it should be a society largely segregated according to sex, as Rousseau was demanding in, for example, the *Lettres à d'Alembert*.[36] Here again it was possible to draw on Montesquieu, who permitted great freedom for women in monarchies, but in republics demanded their subjection to strict laws of morality:

> Les femmes ont peu de retenue dans les monarchies, parce que la distinction des rangs les appellant à la cour, elles y vont prendre cet esprit de liberté qui est à peu près le seul qu'on y tolère [...]. Dans les républiques, les femmes sont libres par les lois, et captivées par les moeurs, le luxe en est banni, et avec lui la corruption et les vices.[37]

The subjection of women to the morality laws was, according to Montesquieu, of such importance for the republics because it was precisely the loss of female virtuousness which posed the greatest threat to this particular form of state:

> Il y a tant d'imperfections attachées à la perte de la vertu dans les femmes, toute leur âme en est si fort dégradée, ce point principal ôté en fait tomber tant d'autres, que l'on peut regarder, dans un état populaire, l'incontinence publique comme le dernier des malheurs, et la certitude d'un changement dans la constitution. Aussi les bons législateurs y ont-ils exigé des femmes une certaine gravité des moeurs. Ils ont proscrit de leurs républiques non seulement le vice, mais l'apparence même du vice. Ils ont banni jusqu'à ce commerce de galanterie qui produit l'oisivité, qui fait que les femmes corrompent avant même d'être corrumpues, qui donne un prix à tous les riens, et rabaisse ce qui est important, et qui fait que l'on ne se conduit plus que sur les maximes du ridicule, que les femmes entendent si bien à établir.[38]

---

36 See Brigitte Schnegg, 'Soireen, Salons, Sozietäten. Geschlechterspezifische Aspekte des Wandels städtischer Öffentlichkeit im Ancien Régime am Beispiel Berns', in Anne-Lise Head, Albert Tanner (eds), *Frauen in der Stadt* (Zürich: 1993), pp. 163–83.

37 Montesquieu, *De l'Esprit des Lois*, Livre VII, Chap. IX.

38 ibid, Chap. VIII.

It has been indicated several times already that Montesquieu was amongst the most widely read authors of the Swiss Enlightenment. His thesis about the dire consequences of female vice accorded with the observations which many a member of the Swiss Enlightenment felt able to make in his own country. There was widespread agreement that the order of the sexes in an ideal republic of the future would have therefore to orientate itself to these handicaps and would have to guarantee the virtuousness of the female sex by a renunciation of luxury, by strict laws on morality, by a large measure of segregation of the sexes in social intercourse and also by appropriate education.

Let us close by taking stock. The designs of the members of the Swiss Enlightenment for the future were in great part backward-looking and were basically oriented on a heroic past. The present, experienced as a crisis, was interpreted again and again as a fall from a good, ancient order. Like Franz Urs Balthasar, who sought for means 'die veraltete Eydgenossschaft wieder zu verjüngen', many hoped that a return to the old virtues would be able to reverse negative developments. The main ideas of the new order were taken from this past and were 'freedom', 'simplicity', 'virtue' and 'strict morality'. 'Ferne sind uns weiche Sitten,/ Ausgefeilte Lüsternheit;/ Nein! Es wohnt in Schweizerhütten/ Einfalt und Genügsamkeit'.[39] With these verses in 'Lied einer glücklichen Republik', Lavater sums up the *bürgerlich* ideal of a virtuous and frugal republic.

Isaak Iselin was a representative of a view which diverged from the mainstream of the Swiss Enlightenment. He distrusted the allegedly ideal situation in the time of his forefathers, and instead hoped for a society whose prosperity and riches would make possible a life in dignity and virtue for its men and women and an optimal development of the arts and sciences. In explicit contrast to Montesquieu, Iselin does not consider virtue to be the basis of a republican or indeed of any other political constitution. He is convinced that it is love which is that basis. Thus, in contrast to his contemporaries critical of society, he believes in the progress of history,

---

39   Johann Kaspar Lavater, 'Lied einer glücklichen Republik', in *Schweizer Lieder*, 3rd improved and expanded edition (Bern: 1768).

and closes his *Geschichte der Menschheit* with a declaration of faith in the future, as solemn as it is hopeful: 'Alsdenn wird die Liebe – das einzige gute Triebrad jeder Verfassung – triumphierend seine seligen Einflüsse über alle Stände ausgiessen'.[40]

Translated by Malcolm Pender

---

40   Isaak Iselin, *Geschichte der Menschheit*, 2nd edition, 1768, vol II, p. 425f., quoted in Im Hof, *Isaak Iselin und die Spätaufklärung*, p. 234.

Contributors

Joy Charnley
Department of Modern Languages
University of Strathclyde
Livingstone Tower
Richmond Street
GB – Glasgow G1 1XH
j.charnley@ccsun.strath.ac.uk

Bernard Degen
Historisches Institut
Universität Bern
Länggassstrasse 49
CH – 3000 Bern 9
bernard.degen@hist.unibe.ch

Armin Kühne
Verwaltungskontrolle des Bundesrates
Marktgasse 52
CH – 3003 Bern
Armin.Kuehne@bk.admin.ch

Malcolm Pender
Department of Modern Languages
University of Strathclyde
Livingstone Tower
Richmond Street
GB – Glasgow G1 1XH
m.j.pender@strath.ac.uk

Fabienne Regard
77 Rte du Chablais
F – 74140 Veigny Foncenex
fregard@internet-montblanc.fr

Brigitte Schnegg
Altenbergstrasse 120
CH – 3013 Bern
schneggvonruette@datacomm.ch

Occasional Papers in Swiss Studies

The Centre for Swiss Cultural Studies in the Department of Modern Languages of the University of Strathclyde in Glasgow (GB) was set up in 1996, formalising a long tradition of publication, research and teaching in Swiss studies there. As part of the expansion of activities in publishing and in creating outlets for scholarly work, it was decided to launch a series, *Occasional Papers in Swiss Studies*. It is envisaged that each volume of the series, which will appear at intervals of about a year, will bring together approximately six essays relating to a single theme written by scholars in the field of Swiss studies. It is the aim of the editors to select themes which have a contemporary dimension and, whilst the majority of the essays will have a literary focus, each number will contain at least one essay by a scholar in a discipline such as history or cultural studies. It is hoped that the series will both present aspects of Swiss culture and contribute to general debate on matters Swiss.

Volume 1   Images of Switzerland – Challenges from the Margins.
            128 pp. 1998.
            ISBN 3-906762-34-3 / US-ISBN 0-8204-4231-3. SFr. 32.–.

Volume 2   Switzerland and War.
            129 pp. 1999.
            ISBN 3-906764-65-6 / US-ISBN 0-8204-4641-6. SFr. 32.–.

Volume 3   Visions of Utopia in Switzerland.
            115 pp. 2000.
            ISBN 3-906766-64-0 / US-ISBN 0-8204-5336-6. SFr. 38.–.